A Postcard Memoir

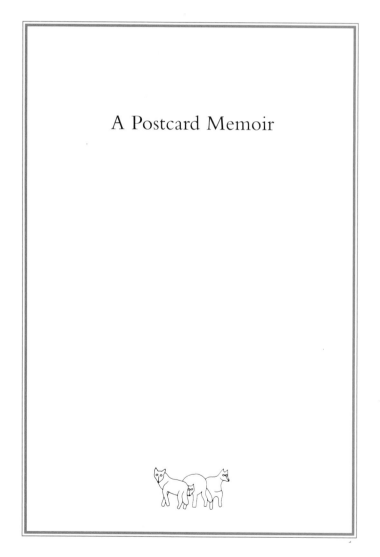

Other books by Lawrence Sutin

Jack and Rochelle: A Holocaust Story of Love and Resistance

Divine Invasions: A Life of Philip K. Dick

Do What Thou Wilt: A Life of Aleister Crowley

A Postcard Memoir

by **Lawrence Sutin**

Graywolf Press

Saint Paul, Minnesota

Publication of this volume is made possible
in part by a grant provided by the Minnesota
State Arts Board through an appropriation by
the Minnesota State Legislature, and by a
grant from the National Endowment for the
Arts. Significant support has also been provided by the Bush Foundation; Dayton's,
Mervyn's and Target stores through the
Dayton Hudson Foundation; the McKnight
Foundation; and other generous contribu-
tions from foundations, corporations, and
individuals. To these organizations and individuals we offer our heartfelt thanks.

Additional funding for this title was provided
by the Jerome Foundation.

Published by Graywolf Press
2402 University Avenue
Suite 203
Saint Paul, Minnesota 55114

www.graywolfpress.org

Published in the United States of America
Printed in Canada

ISBN 1-55597-304-3

2 4 6 8 9 7 5 3 1
First Graywolf Printing, 2000

Library of Congress Catalog Card Number:
99-067243

Cover and interior design: Jeanne Lee

To Mab
my heart

A Postcard Memoir

PROLOGUE

What first caused me to confuse postcards and life was an accidental glance while getting change for a purchase at the Starr Bookshop in Cambridge, Massachusetts, back in 1973. There was a shoe box by the cash register full of old postcards priced a dime apiece. At the front was the postcard of the mosque at Sidi-Okba pictured later in this book.

My glance grew into a stare and then there came a brief mind pop in which I entered the mosque and felt its cool air and the sand-gritted flagstones on my bare baked feet.

I bought that postcard and started to buy more, whatever caught my eye. There was almost a decade during which I stopped because I thought it was getting ridiculous, the clamminess of a collection, and I boxed my postcards up and kept them in the basement. But then they started to appear in my dreams as lost times, lost knowledge, lost children. So I let them out and started to accumulate them again.

Some years ago I learned, by accident, that postcards offered a way to shatter the mirror of the everyday and to enter into whatever I was writing. I would look through a goodly sized pile and, by the time I was done, my brain had chased its tail and I was ready to say what I needed.

It came about that certain memories of mine began to seep into certain postcards, there to remain like bugs in amber. Other postcards challenged me to come out after them and fight like a writer, which I did, realizing, accidentally again, that they were egging me on through the stations of my life.

"Fish Jump—Bonneville Fish Ladder"

When I was a little boy—*who knows how little?*—I was conscious that grown men had once been like me. But they had transformed into fathers of families they took to parks and sights and fed hot dogs and ice cream. It seemed often the case that the kids and the mother enjoyed the fish jumps while Dad kept his eyes up ahead on the bend of the road. Just as I was in tow to my parents, he was in tow to that bend, that future that curved back to being a son. When I was a little boy, I often wanted to hide behind bushes and peek at the world going by. That was better, for me, than seeing the sights. But parents want to know where you are. So what I wanted was to grow up and be free to get lost. Families would always try to find you, and as a dad, you had to let yourself be found. The fathers I saw in parks had been found for good. You could tell by the way they sat on benches waiting for kids to come back with their cones. I didn't know, as a kid watching fathers, that someday I'd jump as high as the fish, that being found once you were lost wasn't so easy.

B-31 Fish Jump - Bonneville Fish Ladder

"Pissed Off at Three Years and Four Months"

One theory of life development is that we are designed never to understand ourselves. Those who think they come to any final understanding are merely sedated, however crystalline their reasons or bloody their faiths. Under this theory I would have no idea why at a very early age, as far back as I can remember there being a me, I was uneasy, easily angered, cognizant of the rankness of adult human odors. I never liked it when adults had a story for me that wasn't from a book. It meant they wanted me to believe something they believed. I couldn't have said it this way then but I knew that my mind was the field of play between us. I was jumbled inside between theirs and mine and only quiet could make it stop. I didn't want to talk back. I was too angry already for that. I wouldn't come out to meet company in the living room if they offered fruit or sugar cookies. I would if they offered chocolate. I would if it was my birthday or Hanukkah and they had presents. I would if my parents came looking for me and insisted. Craven as I was, my parents would kindly give in after I'd made my brief hellos and how are yous and let me hide in the basement where I learned to make sparks pounding nails into the concrete floor hard.

"Jeune Mère"

I was born to a strong and tender and frightened woman. My mother lost her parents and her sisters in the Holocaust. She was gang-raped by Russian partisans in the Polish woods after escaping from the Nazi ghetto established in her hometown of Stolpce. In marrying my father—a Jewish partisan leader who gave her shelter in an underground bunker—she was staking her soul on creating a new family. Her first baby, a boy, died shortly after his premature birth in the fall of 1945. Dread brought on that early delivery. My mother had learned of a pogrom carried out by Poles against those surviving Jews trying to return to their homes in the nearby town of Katowice. "Even after the Germans surrendered, the Poles continued to kill us," my mother told me. She told me everything from the time I was old enough to follow the basic sense, at six or so. I was the third child, after my unnamed dead brother and after my sister, who entered life in a displaced persons camp in Germany in 1947. As to bearing children, my mother knew an old Yiddish saying: "Three is two and two is one." My sister and I were both treated as if we were each the only one, the precious one, the one who could be lost at any time. I came out of my mother's womb on time and healthy in October 1951, the first member of the family born in America. But I was not born into an American home. There was herring, butter, and pumpernickel bread on our breakfast table, along with strong sweet tea. We spoke Yiddish a lot. As a young boy, I would ask Mother what we were having for dinner and she would tell me, *"drek mit leber,"* "shit with liver," meaning don't ask what there will be to eat, be thankful there will be something. When I was born, she remembered, I know, the emaciated lost one laid on the windowsill to die by a small-town Polish physician who had no way to treat him. Mother never wanted to give him a name. I never asked why but I knew that naming him would have made it worse. I was named after her father Lazar, in Hebrew Eliezer, in English Larry. I was one, living for two, and my mother was living for me, but fiercely, tending me like a bruise.

"Man and Boy"

Fathers more easily love their daughters. Sons are the continuation of us in an obvious sense, so obvious that it is unbearable. In the case of my father and myself, I had the fullness of his face and his desire to write, which had been abandoned when he came to America with a family to raise. What he wanted to see in me were the practical choices he had made confirmed. At times in my youth he justly found me clumsy, cowardly, callous, and he let it be known. His anger had, then, the finality of a curse. The great task in the life of a son is to realize that his father is right and then to proceed to be wrong. It's your only chance to become someone you haven't already met. My father also let his love be known. Once he cried because he feared I did not love him back. Lay down on his bed fully dressed in the middle of the day and cried. My mother found me and pulled me by my scruff to the doorway of their bedroom to see. She was hating me so I lay down beside him and hugged him. That was hard. He was a middle-aged man who was sobbing and sweaty and his body was heavy and so soft I imagined his ribs giving way like a snowman's on the first warm winter day. I could hear his heart and it sounded as if it was working harder than it could take. I hugged him until he stopped crying. I whispered in his ear that I loved him.

"Frère et Soeur"

Even my mother says that my sister and I have nothing in common. People say that I look like my father and my sister looks like my mother. I think I look like my mother. People say that personality-wise, my sister is like my father and I'm like my mother. To me, my sister is kind and anxious. To her, I am funny and impatient. We share no interests, don't like the same anything. I am a suspicious intellectual and she's so blandly sentimental. Socially, we get along nicely at what you call family occasions but we don't spend much time alone together. But we're bound together by being their children, the survivors of the survivors. We heard the stories as kids and they got into our dreams, storm troopers breaking down the doors of all our hiding places. We are amongst the very few who realize constantly what can happen and how much our children would need us. There is a code connected to that that only we know and can enforce upon each other. I rebel against the code, which embarrasses me as trauma. But in secret I keep it. On my sister it fits like a space suit she knows she'd be crazy ever to get out of. My parents won't fully die until my sister's time comes.

"Tina and Lani"

After ten years in America, my father saved enough to buy a house in St. Louis Park, a suburb of Minneapolis, west across the Mississippi from St. Paul. But they had left behind their old and only friends. It wasn't so easy to make new friends, given the long hours they worked, given their accents, given the pain that leaked through the small talk my parents came to understand wasn't small but rather all there was. Their old friends were survivors, too, and they understood. They were a frayed and suspicious couple who were fiercely gracious with children, just like my parents were. We often drove back to St. Paul on Sundays to visit with them. They had two daughters, one my sister's age and one born within weeks of me. Tina and Lani. I remember their faces and the grace they possessed without beauty, but nothing they said. We played hide-and-go-seek once and I left the house to hide in the rotting toolshed leaning against the garage. No one found me. I was handling amazing implements of torture—a long-poled weed scythe crescent-shaped to slit a throat, a bow saw with thrusting rusty teeth like a ravenous guard dog with bloody gums, poison sprayers that killed if you didn't wash the tomatoes you picked in the garden, pliers that could rip out your fillings. The toolshed window was broken—you could slice yourself open if you tried to escape that way. I then became afraid that the toolshed door had locked itself behind me. I pushed and it swung open easy as pie. So I closed it again and now I wanted to lock myself in. I could make a world of it in here. I'd noticed the small bags of carrot and pea and cabbage seeds, chewable in measured handfuls. There was a coiled garden hose that was dripping, a sign that in its length there was water to sip. I tried to calculate how many days I'd survive, which was the real trick to hide-and-seek as I saw it.

"Grandfather Before He Was Grandfather"

When I was seven, we moved to a small house on a small hill. I shared a room with my grandfather Julius. Our beds were side-by-side, separated by a wooden table on which he set his glasses at day's end. On the table was a lamp with a green shade. As I grew older, I read late into the night while Grandfather slept, his eyes closed as gently as butterfly wings, his breaths slow and drifting as the curtains in the summer-night breezes. On Saturday mornings, he would sometimes take me to the main Minneapolis library, an old brownstone building with cushioned window seats that were perfect for reading. My grandfather would find large, heavy art books with color plates of the works of the great painters. In those old-fashioned books, only the top edges of the color plates were glued to the pages. You could lift them up, then let them fall like autumn leaves. In those plates I saw St. George kill the dragon, Mary snuggle her child, the fleets of Venice sail the canals—and also ordinary people who faced me directly, as if the paint that made them up was flesh and blood. Julius had gone to art school in Warsaw as a young man. That was fiercely unusual for a Jewish boy raised to believe, by his Orthodox rabbi father, that to paint any living creature, much less a human, was to trespass on the work of creation that belongs to God alone. While in Warsaw, Julius wrote his father a letter that broke contact between them forever. Five decades later, Grandfather would take me with him to the park, where he set up a small easel and a blanket on which I lay down and read while he painted in watercolors that sank into the mottled absorbent paper like waves into sand. The blues of his skies and waters rippled. His clouds were so fleecy it seemed as if I could have poked through them with my finger. But I never would have touched one of Grandfather's paintings.

"Chimère"

I was five years old when I became aware that I was being watched by gargoyles. At first it seemed a bit silly, that's all. But then I realized they were inside me, perched in the grey slimy crannies of my brain. I knew what my brain looked like as I'd seen Bugs Bunny pull out a chart of the brain in a Looney Tunes cartoon in which he was pretending to be a professor. I remember the day I knew the gargoyles would be watching inside me forever. I was on my way to kindergarten, was less than a block from the school. I was being teased by an older boy and I picked up a rock and threw it at him and hit a little girl in the forehead instead. There was a sound like a bat on a ball. The ball was her skull. The bat was my mind and the gargoyles. She screamed. Her mother ran out and pressed a white towel to her brow that turned red. I was led to the principal's office by someone I don't remember. I was scared for myself and the principal said I didn't seem sorry. My mother arrived and talked to the little girl's mother, who showed sympathy for my mother's despair at having a son like me. I had a weak arm, the little girl wasn't badly hurt. So I got off with a lecture I can't remember. The rock striking and the girl screaming is a scene in my head I still can't bear to see. But I do. It's the gargoyles' favorite movie to play when I'm not doing anything worth watching.

73·E.B.   *PARIS. — Notre-Dame. — Chimère. — ND Phot.*

"Capri—Spadaro"

This picturesque old Capriote fisherman posed for a number of postcards in the 1930s, of which I own two. He is the man of the earth with the joys of earth that are simple and ready to hand. The great uncle I got in real life was alive because he had fled from Poland and his own family in the 1930s. As my mother was the daughter of his hated older brother, he helped our family come to America and then treated her like a servant without pay, as was his due since no one had ever helped him. He was a many-time millionaire from real estate bought by the sweat of his brow in the late Depression and held to as tightly as the cane he employed in his stroke-ridden dotage. As he was a miser for lack of other passions, his delight in my mother's High Holidays meals was that they came with seconds and thirds and always for free. He thought of money as soldiers—the more soldiers you had, the more battles you won. He liked to smoke cigars because they took up the whole room. When I was born, this is true, I peed in the face of his wife when she peered over infant me in the hospital. Their only child, a daughter, died young.

My great uncle died around that time, too, but his wife lived to ninety-six. My mother invited her to everything and she took up her late husband's place as the bloated feted elder. On one occasion, when she saw my mother in the same blouse she herself was wearing, she demanded that my mother change her outfit at once. My great aunt asked me once, as I was driving her back to her plush senior-living-community condo after some family dinner, if I would say Kaddish for her at her graveside once she was gone. I told her I would. To get even with her for making me toady like that— like my mother had for fifty years—I didn't so much as attend her funeral, which made me uneasy but even so.

Capri - Spadaro

"Star of Bethlehem Home"

As a boy I loved being places I wasn't supposed to be—alleys, back roads, abandoned lots, decaying buildings, hidden driveways. I rode my red bike hard looking for adventure on those summer afternoons. I pretended my bike was an Appaloosa horse. When I'd come to a stop at a traffic light, I'd pat down its frame and fenders, saying, "Whoa boy," softly. When the light turned green I'd give it a quick light kick with my sneaker heel to signify time to gallop. Then we'd veer off to the side streets, to the forgotten places where a boy on his bike could slip into and past. Once I found a railroad yard with empty, open freight cars that I climbed up into and found hay, cow shit, brown beer bottles, and empty Spam cans with twist keys. The cans were so clean—I bent down and checked, the way cowboys fingered and sifted campfire ash to tell how long since the bad guys had left the site—I figured it had to be cats and rats at work, which made me scared so I jumped down and back on my bike. In the process I fell and scored my knee on gravel through my jeans, so I pedaled home like a cavalry scout weak from an arrow wound. One day, riding around on the prairie, I took an alley and an open-gated driveway to a building high up on what I called a butte. It was the Star of Bethlehem Home. I tethered my horse to a bush and walked slowly toward the main door sheltered by a columned portico. I looked in and there, in a kind of lobby, were only old people, some in bathrobes and housecoats, others in dungarees, plaid shirts, and suspenders or white silk blouses with black or grey skirts and pearls around their necks and in their ears. Some were white and pink with soft hair on their heads like bunnies. Some were sitting, parts of them perfectly still, parts of them shaking. No one saw me. Then a trim younger man in a white uniform, both medical and nautical, came from behind the reception desk with a tray filled with little paper cups. Some of the old people wanted their cup-treats and some of them shied away toward tall red velvet curtains big enough to hide behind. This younger man noticed me and his face changed into a lit fuse. He headed toward the door and I bolted across the lawn, jumped on my bike, not daring to look back, bent over the handlebars and whispered into its ear, "C'mon boy, let's ride! We've got to get back to the fort to let the captain know that the Kickapoos, Cheyennes, and Apaches have all gathered here for a war powwow."

STAR OF BETHLEHEM HOME
ST. LOUIS PARK, MINN.

"Fairchild Tropical Garden"

My fifth-grade teacher took our class on a tour of a potato-chip factory. Her uncle was a manager there and made sure we got the best treatment— a free bag of Red Dot Chips for each of us, along with a red Red Dot baseball cap, a red Red Dot balloon, and a red round Red Dot plastic change purse you squeezed to open and close. We saw crates of potatoes poured into machines that washed, peeled, sliced, and sent the glistening discs on conveyor belts to boiling vats of oil. We saw fried chips draining and drying. The men and women who worked there were so covered with grease—it misted the air—that they seemed ready for frying themselves. Not doing what they had dreamed of doing as children, they took no pleasure in being observed by us. They understood that we kids were hoping we would never be them. Our teacher had arranged the tour to get herself out of the classroom in which her own dream was dying. She had always wanted to be beloved by her students. But none of us did love her—her gestures were stiff, her voice failed in the after-noons, her eyes wandered out the windows as often as ours did. Now, in the chip factory, as our cheeks swelled and reddened from humidity and oil, she nibbled at a new strategy, displaying the consequences of indifference to teachers and their lessons. You grew up and took readings on grease vats while kids watched.

"The Fairchild Rambler" which makes tour of the garden. Fairchild Tropical Garden.

"Welsh National Costume"

When I was seven, just after we moved from St. Paul to St. Louis Park, from an urban brownstone apartment to a suburban house, my sister decided she wanted a dog. I hadn't ever thought about it. There was an old lady down the street who had a downscale kennel business going on in her basement and backyard—her whole house, really, as her whole house smelled of dog, dog food, dog pee, and dog powdered-liver nutritional supplement. Her name was Mrs. Small. We got the dog from her, a white cocker spaniel pup with golden spots named Peaches and Cream, Peaches for short. Perhaps Peaches was weaned too soon, or the smell of Mrs. Small's house was too strong, or Peaches was never happy with us, or all three. Because every chance Peaches got, she ran away to Mrs. Small, who would come by and let us know, always very gracious, but always with that neatly tucked small smile that was her delight at being loved by Peaches more than we were. I was slow to adore Peaches but I finally did, the start of a lifetime of loving crazy damn dogs. It hurt to have Peaches run away. To avoid facing that small smile again I'd chase after Peaches with a slimy slice of baloney in my hand, crying out her name to get her to notice the meat. Once I tried sitting down in the road, holding my ankle as if it was hurt so she would come save me like Lassie did on TV. Coulda died doing that. Think of it. Kids.

Welsh National Costume

"Merchants"

My grandfather took care of me while my parents both worked in the family gift business. Grandfather was calm and kind but also old and sleepy. Especially in winter, when shadows filled the house like rising water in the late afternoons while Grandfather snored, I was unnerved. My sister was older and talked on the phone in her own upstairs room. In the den above the garage, sitting in my father's home-office swivel chair, the TV on as the only light, I would wait for my parents to come home. Because my grandfather couldn't cook I was encouraged to call a delivery place called "Chicken Delight" for dinner whenever I wanted. My mother would leave money for me on the kitchen table, always including a nice tip for the delivery guy who was almost never the same guy, so it couldn't have been a great job. I liked the french-fried shrimp plate with french fries and coleslaw and beet red cocktail sauce in little plastic packets that I bit open, one by one, and squirted into a dipping pile. Everything was disposable so there were no dishes to wash. I'd eat in the swivel chair and wait for the lights of the golden Olds to turn into the driveway. I would see them and then slip away from the window and turn on a light and pick up a book as if I were OK. When they came home, they were nervous and tired but happy to see me safe and with cocktail sauce on my face. My father would sit at his desk in the chair I'd been in just minutes before, scanning bills and smoking a cigar. Now I felt comfortable going to my room alone to read.

"Summer Girls"

Oh, the summer girls. Oh, the days of trying to pose and use my body like a natural man of the earth so as to draw their eyes. Playing baseball while girls watched was a different kind of baseball altogether. It was as if there were major-league scouts sitting in the stands (the shaded hill behind the backstop) assessing our genetic skills and sexual hustle. Yes, the summer girls talked amongst themselves, sometimes ignored the play, often wandered off to their own backyard gatherings in which dolls and fleecy pets held sway. Still, they were taking us in with precision and passion, even if that precision was instinct and that passion was scorn.

SUMMER GIRLS
AT ANNANDALE MINN.

"Hennebont. La Lande des Trois Pierres"

I had three buddies when I was a little boy. We looked off in different directions but still hung out together. There was a loyalty between us while it lasted, a code that broke with puberty. I would not like to see them again, and the same is true for them, I'm sure. But back then, yes, on summer-vacation mornings we'd meet at the park on our bikes, play baseball, pedal to the drug store for comic books and candy, find a go-cart frame and rig up an old lawn-mower engine to power it weakly. There was a swamp in which we constructed hidden forts, a vacant lot for rock fights with other boys from a block or two farther away. We shot pool in basement rec rooms, tried to make a pet of a wild baby squirrel and carried it tucked up the sleeves of our hero jackets. We watched some TV, had moms make us snacks, phoned the neighborhood grocery store and asked the owner if he had pickled pigs' feet and laughed and hung up when he said he did, get it? We traded baseball cards, set up a spooky attic one Halloween with ketchup oozing out the sockets of a plastic skull, even had some parties toward the end at which we slow danced with girls. Then we all changed. One of us joined a gang, one of us got cute and popular, one of us found a girlfriend he stayed with and later married, one of us was better off being alone for a while, or so he says now, the water of that time having run through his fingers.

2202. - HENNEBONT. - La Lande des Trois Pierres

France

"La Salle de la Melpomène"

No quibbling over truth, not here. *Memory is not merely selective. It is also tutelary, oracular. It is, in the end, as reliable as we are.* The names and facts of my life as names and facts are insignificant. What we call history is something I slipped through. My life as I remember it to be is all I have to live on. I remember it as a plunge underwater, as a kite baffled and frantic in the wind, as a country-night sky pouring into my head every star, as smells of basements and bathrooms and black earth and lilacs and coffee and sex, as a hatred of mirrors, as a discarding of weighty thought, as stillness and persistence. All I know is of these things or states and how they made me feel. That would be truth in this book.

732 PARIS. — *Musée du Louvre*. — *La Salle de la Melpomène* — LL.

"A Bunch of Sky Scrapers"

This was roughly the view out of my doctor's window while I was a kid waiting in one of his little treating rooms with my pants down (at the request of the departing female nurse) for him to come in and give me a shot. He was a cocksure old man who had patients who'd been seeing him for forty years.

My parents worshipped him because he could talk a bit of Yiddish and readily ticked off the worst possibilities for any symptoms brought to his attention. Worst possibilities were something my parents felt comfortable with. With my sister and myself, it was pretty much routine maintenance: booster shots, tonsils out, sewing up a jagged cut in my right leg. He had a busy practice and when he came in to give me a shot he didn't like to answer questions or coddle my slight squirmy fear. Even as I tried to talk he would place his hand on the back of my head, bend me down over the tissue-covered treatment table, swab and stab and tell me I could pull up my pants. Only then would he ask how it was going with me as he disposed of the syringe and washed his hands. Once, when I was maybe in sixth grade, I told him I wanted to be a writer. He shook his head in pity. "Can't stand the sight of blood, eh?" he said as he went out the door with his sweaty bald head, rolled-up sleeves, hairy arms, tweedy vest, and pants. I doubted he noticed the view from his treating rooms. I envied him.

A BUNCH OF SKY SCRAPERS
MINNEAPOLIS MINN

"The Leamington Hotel"

For a couple of years in the early 1960s, after the Washington Senators moved to Minnesota to become the Twins, I used to take the bus to the downtown hotels where I knew the visiting baseball teams stayed. You could get autographs in the lobbies when the players passed through. It was easy to spot them even if you didn't recognize them from their cards because they dressed like Arrow Shirt ads and were in good shape, unlike the businessmen who stayed in the hotel, too. The slugger Rocky Colavito, then with the Athletics, was right to remind me gruffly that, though I'd asked nicely for him to sign, I should also have said "thank you" when he handed my book back. Oriole second-baseman Jerry Adair was obviously happy when I told him I'd seen a home run he hit on TV. Announcer Joe Garagiola said to a group of us boys by the elevator: "Don't you ever sleep?" He signed my book but I'd never ask him again. Yankee shortstop Tony Kubek told us that if we wanted to grow up to be good players we needed to play a lot. The ultimate Yankee of my time, Mickey Mantle, seemed a little embarrassed and wrote beautiful M's that looked to me like butterflies. An old coach I lucked onto signed his name "Luke Appling," which made him the White Sox shortstop from the 1930s to the 1950s whose famous baseball nickname was "Old Aches and Pains." He looked just that standing there before me ten years after his achy playing days were over. My kid brain was staggered for the first time by how life could stretch out and and what it might feel like when things finally started to snap. Gates Brown of the Tigers, a middling outfielder who could hit, was short but so muscled I was all the more amazed. Indians southpaw Sudden Sam McDowell gripped the pen as if he were setting to throw the curve. His teammate, righty Luis Tiant, spoke in the first Cuban accent I'd ever heard outside of Desi Arnaz on TV. Why did I go to those hotels and why did I stop? These days autographs are worth money but I didn't know or care about that back then. Best I can say, I wanted to make sure those guys were real since I so avidly fantasized about being one of them. But two years and dozens of autographs later it had become both a job and a lie. That's what Rocky Colavito saw straight off, that I said "please" when I approached but not "thank you" when I got what I wanted. That's like a hitter guessing fastball right and then not bothering to swing. Colavito led the American League in home runs one year. He could size up big-league pitchers, so figuring out when a kid needed a new fantasy was no sweat.

The Leamington Hotel - Minneapolis, Minn. 3rd Ave., 10th to 11th St.

"Baseball Team"

My baseball career ended when I was fourteen. Oh, I horsed around with beery softball after that, but the days of putting on a wool uniform with matching cap, stirrup socks and cleats, of breaking in a glove through the winter by oiling it, slamming a ball into the pocket and binding the whole with rubber bands to make it cupped and pliant for spring, those days were gone. In my final Pony League season I batted .308 with a homer, way better hitting than the coach's son produced. But the coach's son was fast and could cover center while I lumbered in right. I kept asking to switch to first base as I loved watching Vic Power play it like a lunging sword fight for the Twins. Finally one night, the coach, who was sick of us all, son included, for losing decided to stick me at first, saying, "Don't make me look stupid." Our regular first baseman was sent to right field. He jogged past me as I was throwing practice grounders to the infield and mentioned that I was a fuckhead. I played a decent game and dived to knock down a ball heading down the line to prevent extra bases. Next game I was in right again. I jogged past the regular who'd reclaimed first and told him he'd sucked coach's dick just right. He said, yeah, your sister taught me how. Fifth inning there was a foul pop deep behind first. I charged it, screaming him off, and dropped it. Played out the season on grit, left the game the right way, before it left me.

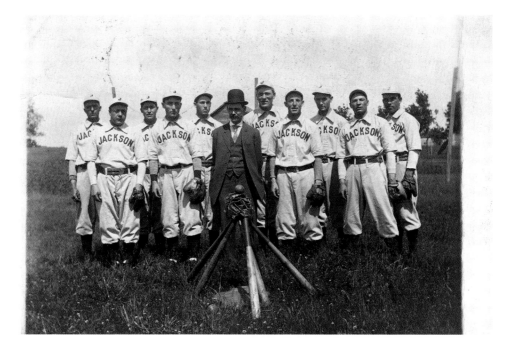

"Ismaël"

I'd say I was five when a picture of a woman first captured my attention. It was the dancer Cyd Charisse in a magazine ad for stockings. Eight years passed. Another picture captured my attention: a young Raquel Welch in a bikini in *LIFE*. I went to my room with *LIFE*. I didn't close the door, as I didn't know what I was about to do. Like an otter catching its first fish, I lay stomach-down on my bed, holding the glossy page up in the sunlight. Then I started to wriggle. No hands. I had never before been so conscious of my blood in its courses through my body. There were sudden heaving heights of bloated nausea, tepid reliefs when I slowed, which was not for long. The feeling down there controlled my mind more directly than anything ever. It could have been God in my penis. I writhed like a snake on its belly, abandoned by its father but determined to live. Twice before I came I thought I'd better stop, I'll hurt myself, I'll break it. The end was eyes shut, a shuddering smashup, a cold puddle under my belly. I can't remember how I cleaned up or if I tried again that day but it was soon, very soon, it had to have been. I've never told a soul until now.

Musée du Luxembourg
34 — Jules BECQUET. *Ismaël.* *ND Phot.*

"Herzl"

As my Bar Mitzvah approached, it became necessary for me to learn to sing my Hebrew haftorah, or selection from the Prophets, that would form part of the Sabbath service at which I would become a man. My teacher for this task was a part-time cantor named Petrokin who supplemented his income in this way. He had sung and recorded all the haftorahs, and each of his students purchased, for home practice, his 45 rpm record for their particular prophet. Mine was Obadiah, whom I have never heard mentioned since. On his record, Cantor Petrokin sounded like Perry Como, but stiff, not relaxed like Perry. In person, Petrokin was stiffer still. He gave lessons at home in a little den with walls covered with old photos of Jewish men who looked like him, but with beards. I asked once, just after a lesson, why he didn't have one. Cantor Petrokin already knew I had no voice. That made me a tiresome student, and I could see his surprise at my having noticed something, anything. Maybe that's why he answered me: "My father came from Russia where a boy grew a beard as soon as he was Bar Mitzvahed. So God commanded. But I had nothing to shave until I was twenty. By then my father was dead. For God alone to grow a beard I could not bring myself to do. Besides," and here Petrokin winked man to man, "Jewish girls in America liked clean faces."

401

45

"Monte-Carlo—Un Coin des Terrasses"

I never aspired to elegance. I never thought it was mine to have. I would have needed the body of my comic-book hero Plastic Man to stretch posture, wardrobe, coiffeur, and calm hint of smile into dazzling alignment, a solar eclipse deceptively searing to the unprotected eye. That was what elegance meant to me. And if you were not elegant, if you were merely wearing and grooming as you were told to wear and groom, then you were stuck in the human race and it didn't much matter, so I thought, where you finished in that race. I was wrong about that, as it turned out. Any distraction that could set you ahead and apart from the rest—from clothing to gold to beauty to indifference—mattered every day to everyone, everywhere. When they insisted they didn't really care and felt themselves as one, it got so I thought I could hear, faintly beneath the bubbles of their words, the starting gun for a new race with the same old finish line. While elegance remained the gift of the gods. Elegance, I learned, extended beyond the person to include locale and context and movement and, most elegant of all, stillness, not fidgeting to get away from being seen. Even elegant people can't help but stop and look at each other. Inside their minds they lick each other like scrumptious ice-cream cones that would otherwise melt and be wasted, so who could blame them? We could, but we do the same thing, so we don't.

MONTE-CARLO. — *Un Coin des Terrasses.*

1294

ND. Phot.

SQUIRRELS NEST POINT
LAKE WASHINGTON
MANKATO, MINN.

"Squirrel's Nest Point"

In my early teens the whole family went to a summer lodge by a lake for a week. We had our own cabin but there were common meals with other guests in the sprawling lodge house that also, on the final Saturday night, offered live entertainment. There were rowboats you could take out on the lake but my father couldn't swim and didn't know how to fish. During the week I mostly swam in the pool and drank Cokes in the snack-bar area alongside the pool. I remember "Summer in the City" by the Lovin' Spoonful on the radio tended by the teenage boy who was the son of the owner of the lodge. He was practiced at dealing with guests. Girls liked him, boys wanted to be like him, adults left him free to goof off. His chest was smoothly rippled like a shoreline rock; he liked to smile; his blond hair was starting to grow long. That was enough, that was plenty. He was friendly with me and showed me some tricks to win free games on the pinball machine. I passed the remaining time reading *The Count of Monte Cristo,* which I liked because it told how to escape the full impact of the random bolts of evil life would have in store for me. My mother couldn't get over the ample baskets of lodge-baked muffins and rolls provided at every meal. The muffins had sliced orange peel in them. My mother wanted me and my sister to eat and eat them. We did. I remember gulping down ice water the old waitress kept refilling. My cheeks were tomato red from the sun and when I touched them the nerves hummed inside my head. Then came Saturday night and I was off my guard. Our dinner table was close to the lodge-house stage, and the entertainer named Jerry sang songs and told jokes, accompanied by a pianist, the owner himself. The songs were showbiz standards like "Fly Me to the Moon" and "Send In the Clowns." The jokes were clean in language for the kids and dirty and weary in essence for the adults. At some point Jerry looked straight at me and said, didn't ask, "Don't you ever smile?" That got a bigger laugh than his jokes. The audience eyes all around me, lit by dinner candles, glittered like the sun had on the pool water all week. I was stuck in my chair, a boy in a body I didn't like to look at in the mirror. My parents laughed as if they thought it was funny the entertainer had spotted me, grumpy as usual, in a crowd like that. My sister said, "Larry, you really could smile." No, I could not. A few minutes later, while Jerry moved on to impressions of John Wayne and Kirk Douglas, I snuck away to the cabin and finished *The Count of Monte Cristo*. To this day, I make it a rule to finish books I take on vacation and to take only books that offer plans of escape if vacations go wrong. To this day, I smile for no one who asks. I don't even say "cheese."

"One of the Men in the White Coats"

veryone has a science-teacher story. Here's mine. It was during the eighth grade, the most painfully raw year of my life. I was changing into an adolescent in public, before my fellow schoolmates. The girls ignored me and the boys used me as a benchmark to gauge how much further they had progressed in physique and sophistication. I was challenged to fights I did not fight. I tried to dress right and had my cool, back-of-the-neck shirt loops ripped routinely when I walked down the hall between classes. When she finally tired of resewing them, my mother simply clipped them off, which felt something like circumcision. As for my teachers at school, I had drawn a spectacularly wretched bunch. My English teacher spent two months on "The Great Stone Face" by Nathaniel Hawthorne, on which I wrote eight tersely lunatic essays, all of which she graded B+. My economics teacher had a smoking habit so intense that he would sit in a glazed trance by the end of the period, waiting like a Pavlovian dog for the bell that would free him to run to the janitorial closet where he kept his smokes until the school hoods began to steal them. But my science teacher was of an altogether different feather. He understood nascent teens with the same precision and indifference as he understood taxonomy. He tossed his scientific knowledge at us with a contempt to which he was entitled in the face of our boredom and scorn. He always wore white gloves and the rumor had passed from year to year that the middle glove finger of his right hand was a fake to mask its loss in a forbidden experiment gone very wrong in his college days. To check that out I constantly watched his right hand. But there was never a definitive movement, or lack thereof, by which I could tell—not that any of my classmates asked for my opinion. As he called on us by pointing (with his index finger) rather than by name, it was a considerable shock to hear him say at the end of the hour (which was also the end of the school day) that Larry Sutin should stay after class. My fellow students smirked or avoided my eyes as they filed out. I walked up to his desk. He raised his right hand in a fist. "This is the only thing that interests you, yes?" I said nothing as he slowly uplifted the middle finger. "See?

Now shake." He grabbed my right hand with his and squeezed until my eyes began to water. I didn't think of screaming. It was his room, his school, his hand, his finger biting into mine. "But how can you be sure," he continued, "it's not a padded metal spring in there? Now there's a question. Can you think of an experiment to answer it?" He let go of me, slapped his hand flat on the desk next to a scalpel of the type we used on frogs. "If you cut through the glove and blood spurted out you'd know, wouldn't you?" I closed my eyes to make it all go away. He pressed the scalpel handle into my hand. "Do it. Now!" I opened my eyes. With his left hand he guided my right to the glove finger. I dropped the scalpel. He took it and sliced. The blood and I both ran.

"Italien. Aufnahmen"

I was fifteen and some of the baby fat had found its way off and I was serious and dreamy, nothing if not those. Emerson wrote that you should beware of what you want for you might get it. There was this overnight-camp social thing held by a Jewish Zionist youth group, Habonim, and a same-age friend of mine was the president of the group. He wore dark blue open-collar shirts and a white-and-blue scarf around his neck and jeans and water-buffalo sandals from India. The big compliment in this group was to call someone *halutzik,* Hebrew for pioneering, in the earthy way the founders of the collective farm *kibbutzim* in Israel had been. As for the Zionism part, none of the group wound up living in Israel. The only person from my high school class who did was a girl who got pregnant by an Israeli soldier. I was intimidated by the photos of the female Israel soldiers I saw in *LIFE.* They carried Uzis and smiled, they could do both and be pretty, that was the point. They weren't going to fall in love with me, but was anyone ever? On the bus to the Habonim overnight a Shoshanna came on to me. She was skinny with glasses and started to kiss me. If I hadn't watched TV I wouldn't have known what she was doing. I kissed back because it was sex I was getting. Her tongue was a wet wiggly worm in my mouth and I was dying to stop. We kissed more, late that night, behind the cabin after the Israeli folk dancing.

"A Scene in 'The White Sister' Act II"

The priest here is talking to Giovanni, a soldier wounded in the Great War, who returned to his Italian hometown to find his wife, who had believed him killed, in the white robes of a nun. The priest is thus posing the question in the dual form of a solace to Giovanni and a quiet insistence upon the sanctity of convent vows as fully equivalent to that of earthly marriage. But wait! We learn that Angela has taken, as her holy name, Sister Giovanna. Further, when questioned by the priest as to why her visits to her husband persist, Sister Giovanna replies: "'Tis my vocation to be near the wounded." Twist upon twist, love in a careen, souls as tender as solitary candles, a starstruck crush on the leading lady (no matter who) from the thirty-seventh row—that was theatre to me as a young teen. I would take in student-discount matinees at the Guthrie after bicycling along the Minneapolis lakes and locking my red Schwinn just outside the theatre entrance. I already knew that I would enter the world of the stage someday. What I would have given to slip past the curtain after the final bow and ovation, to watch the players strip themselves of their costumes and makeup, to ascertain which were happy to be done with mere acting and which lived only for the next performance. I would have told the actor playing Giovanni to give this answer to the casuistic priest: "You're damn right I would! No church, no God, no conceptual trinket of human conscience can or should overcome the happiness of two true lovers!" The actress who had played Sister Giovanna would overhear me and emerge from her dressing room as a lank-haired secular beauty. And we'd go off . . . it was usually a park. We would lie together on the grass and talk and pick little flowers and put them in each other's hair. Like that.

"If Angela had married another man believing you dead,
would you expect the law to annul that marriage so she might
become your wife?"

A SCENE IN "THE WHITE SISTER"   ACT II
Metropolitan, St. Paul, March 25, 26, 27

"Lumber Exchange Building"

This is the building my father worked in from the time that I was seven until I left home for college. He was on the top floor, the founder of a wholesale business named after my mother, Rochelle's, Inc. He leased warehouse, showroom, and office space. His merchandise was not lumber but "Gifts From Around The World," as his cards and catalogues said. In his first years he imported from India, Afghanistan, Austria, Italy, West Germany, France, Japan. As time went on, Taiwan and Hong Kong took prominence. From fine cut-glass crystal, sterling silver lighters, and hand-painted porcelain plates, he downshifted to flocked bunny coin banks, executive mahogany yo-yos, notepads in the shapes of hands and feet, jiggling plasticine creatures called "Boogers" that hung on rearview mirrors. Crap sold at far higher volume than quality, my dad learned. People wanted cheap gifts to give that got an immediate reaction. Chain stores valued my father's ability to pick winning gift lines. They allocated him his own tables in stores and he set up displays to look and sell right. He'd go from store to store in the Twin Cities area on weekends doing that. I never liked my dad's business. When I looked at what he sold, my head would spin. You could live without any of it. What if people ran out of money to waste? It galled him that I never wanted to take the business over. Rochelle's, Inc. wasn't something he could sell. It was based on his own life knowledge and that could only be transmitted to his son if the son were willing. If I had things to do downtown I would visit my father on the top floor. The building had been, in its day, a cathedral of commerce. The hallway floors were marble, as were the urinals. There was ornate ceiling tin and woodwork whitewashed over. My father's office had high fluorescent lights that glared on his growing baldness. He pored over invoices, supervised boys just a few years older than me in packing and shipping the orders. They loved him because he would pay them a little extra when they were broke or in trouble. Together they would ride the creaking freight elevator, taking in, sorting, checking, and shelving new inventory. I would read or listen to Twins games on the radio. No matter what I did, it would hurt him. There was no way I could pretend. I'd ask questions about the business we both knew were stupid. We'd drive home together. At the wheel of the Olds he looked especially exhausted.

2539 Lumber Exchange Building, Minneapolis

"Bacco"

ometimes he appears a boy so beautiful I search my body like a ruins for signs such grace was possible. He is the twiceborn. He tells me that life and death are not all. Something happens in the span that matters. It isn't just eating, sleeping, shitting, fretting. Vegetation and genetalia conjoin into living soul. The brain, a barometer of joy, registers secret happiness in the glad passing to dust. Teenaged, I drank from a jug of red wine sitting in the backseat of my friend's Chevy overlooking the Mississippi. The wine tasted like clay, vinegar, rust. I was trying to get myself drunk, as if I were trying to seduce myself. My friend was laughing at me so shit-faced for the first time ever. The stars over the Mississippi bounced and rolled like diamond dice across the black velvet table of the universe. Some grew huge and caught fire and then fell straight down on me. I told my friend and he stopped laughing and watched my face. It was so beautiful being splashed by fire that I left off talking. Later, so late we spied the false dawn, he drove me home. On his suggestion, I puked in the street rather than in my parents' house. Wine never did anything like that for me again. These days I drink a glass to fall asleep.

FIRENZE - Museo Nazionale - Bacco: Michelangiolo.   286

"Une Ouled Nail"

Before I met the woman I thought I would love forever, I was in love with a girl in high school who looked just like her. There is a dark, serene, haunted look that in those days enchained me at once. I first saw this girl when she was a junior starring in the class play and I was a sophomore sitting in the audience. She played the part of an aspiring actress. I was swept under by her look, those doleful passionate eyes, black hair like the cloak of night, and the faint smile of the new moon. I fantasized about the two of us sitting in the same room together, reading books, watching the sunset out the window, kissing with the slow, precise passion reserved for the spiritually chaste. As to what would have happened had we so much as held hands, it never came up. She had a boyfriend who was slim and offhandedly esoteric with red faun curls that hung over his forehead. At last my stumble-tongued, blushing helplessness won her attention. She took to talking to me now and then, letting me down easy with pointedly casual chitchat. But years later I met her younger brother who burst out laughing when he realized who I was. Behind the scenes of her life I'd made myself a fool. And so I was. Most of the time I'd spent with her was in my own head. She wrote in my yearbook when she graduated and I stayed behind: "What is important, you will remember." I guess it was important then.

"Point No Point"

In the two years before I got my driver's license at sixteen, I used to ride my bike to a lake (there were five near enough) and sit and read. Everything I read had to do with spiritual issues. There was Sartre's *Nausea* with a cover photo of a nauseated naked man touching his breastbone. I felt as though people walking by were noticing me reading that and thinking I was smart and strange. There was Hesse's *Siddhartha* with a cover photo of a smiling, sculpted Buddha. The late-in-life wisdom of Siddhartha that parents should regard a child as a temporary guest in their home struck me deeply, as did the loss of the self. I imagined myself looking so absorbed in my reading that the people passing by would think I was holy. There was Mann's *Death in Venice* and I hadn't yet known that old men could fall in love with boys and die from it. Dead or not, I envied the protagonist his worldwide writerly fame and couldn't feel sorry for him. There was Camus's *The Stranger* but I didn't understand why a casual murderer was innocent just because he didn't need a motive or repentance. What if he had killed my father? I would have killed him back and felt fine about it. That would be innocence. There was Rilke's *Letters to a Young Poet,* which I read to impress the dark actress who held Rilke dear. I wanted to be sensitive like Rilke, who died from the prick of a rose, but tough, too. For me, sensitive was awfully easy.

"POINT NO POINT" ON LAKE PEPIN, MAIDEN ROCK, WIS. 4

"Asta Westergaard"

In high school, a girl named Asta was the one I most desired. I did not adore her—my heart still belonged to another. But Asta would have been welcome to everything else. She was a happy soul with a bouncy athletic body and she made waves with boys and enjoyed it the way a funny person enjoys being funny. Why not? If she was herself lustful, she didn't show it. Asta talked to the boys with the calm, cooing voice you'd use to settle a horse. She smiled at nearly every one of us and lots of us thought we might be her secret one. Once, while playing tennis, I saw Asta and one of her girfriends waiting for our court. She noticed that I saw her and smiled. I played furiously and creamed my opponent, went to the net and graciously shook the loser's hand, then walked toward Asta with my towel draped over my neck in what I thought was a French look. She said, "Good for you, Larry," as I passed by. I said, "Have a good game yourself," and got on my bike. That night in my room I decoded our talk and decided it might be time. I called her house after four times hanging up before the final number. Asta's dad answered, said she wasn't home. He didn't ask for me to leave my name, didn't like me, didn't like the damn boys calling—all that was clear from the spitting tone of his words. How long a line was it to Asta, I wondered. I slept on it. In the morning I gave up and ignored her at school that day.

"Laplandish Dreams"

The woman I thought I would love forever was the older sister of a younger girl who had a crush on me. I wasn't interested in the one I could have had. But the older sister bewitched me. I was seventeen, three years her junior, a brutal gulf at a time in life when every year is the shucking of a skin. One night I walked down the street where she lived and looking up at her lit, curtained window felt like singing the song in *My Fair Lady,* a musical I had thought I hated. The woman I would love forever was small but not frail, had long black hair and dusky skin and a way of passing through the world that was both reverent and removed. I wanted to join her in that. She read the best books, played the piano modestly well, and when I could catch her attention (for she saw me as her sister's catch) she seemed to take my questions and comments more seriously than I did, which was thrilling, a confirmation that I might come out of the room in my head at last and risk baring my soul. Plainly she was destined to be my muse, helpmeet, passion, spur. I had to figure out a way to make her fall in love with me. Then summer ended. She went back to her prestigious Eastern school. Three years would pass before we met again, a half a world away.

"Wonderland"

I remember riding in the car, a kid, to the amusement park. It wasn't just fun I was heading for. My life was going to change for the hours I was there. The fun-house entrance featured wooden planks that moved back and forth to keep you in place so you needed to accelerate. Once in, there were mirrors I wasn't afraid of. They made you wider and shorter, thinner and taller, anything but me. Then came a maze and then the whirling polished wooden disc you sat on and slid off as you got going. There was a big box of gunny sacks to grab from as you went up the steps to the top of the four-lane rippling wooden slide, which was scarier for me than a roller coaster because I went down head first. You could stay in the fun house as long as you wanted. My parents were happy to wait on the bench outside. And when I came out they bought me my two favorites, caramel corn and sno-cones, both of which were food forms I never had anywhere else. Then I would ride the Tilt-a-Whirl, the Wheeling Star, the Cyclone. Years went by and I didn't go back to the amusement park until the summer after my junior year in high school. I'd just gotten my driver's license and came out one night on a whim because I'd heard the park's days were numbered. The land was going to be converted to condos.

Everyone who goes back to something they loved as a kid has to see how small and old it's gotten. I bought a ticket for the fun house and walked the planks in my normal stride and still got in and passed by the mirrors without looking and watched the kids on the disc then tried the slide but had to duck going up the stairs and took up two lanes going down. Once out, I bought fries and a root beer and found a dark bench under a tree. Then I saw two of my high school classmates, a short smart-ass guy with thick brown hair in a forelock bob like the hamburger Big Boy, and the girl he had his arm around, a pretty German blond with orchid blue eyes and a figure that was just filling out. I watched them walk, so together their butts bumped, to the ticket window for the Cyclone. And then I watched them go up the steps and the wooden ramp to the top car, which was maybe forty feet above me. The Cyclone was a ride that went round and round in a circle pressing you back into the person behind you. He got in first and then she sat down between his legs and wiggled and giggled while the operator belted them in. The ride started and they were a blur but it's still, for me, a lonely ecstasy.

1500 Wonderland, Minneapolis.

"Kind of a Jaunty Guy"

I met Marshall in the eighth grade. We were in the same English class and both wanted to be writers. He was cuter and more confident but I was as funny and had the stranger mind. As thespians, we were both somewhat right for the same parts in school plays year after year. He got the parts with joy to them because he was happier than I was. Junior year in *You Can't Take It with You,* Marshall got to be made up in ludicrous blackface makeup as happy butler "Charlie" while I was in a boring business suit as the boring father-in-law-to-be whose daughter loves the wild and crazy family that I had the right to belong to, too. Senior year I was editor of the school paper and he was the insubordinate feature editor. He assigned himself stories that allowed him to meet Paul Simon and Frank Zappa while I was having an existential crisis, losing faith in the value of anything less anguished than Baudelaire. I wasn't reading the pieces I was supposed to be editing anymore. I just scanned them looking for typos I could correct to show by red pencil that I'd passed by at least. I caught hell from the faculty adviser. That same senior year, Marshall and I were in *Death of a Salesman,* Marshall as good-time neighbor "Charlie" and me as rich and powerful "Uncle Ben," the unrepetentant Marley's ghost to Willy Loman's failed Scrooge. Marshall turned in a solid performance playing someone much like himself. I was a disaster as "Uncle Ben." I was afraid of that fierce commerce-conquering character and couldn't speak his lines without feeling them directed to myself as the failed salesman of my own life. By this time, Marshall and I had become friends based on the tacit understanding that adolescence was a competitive event he had won. The summer after senior year, Marshall dyed a white T-shirt, white pants, white socks, and white sneakers all orange, took acid, and swore that his deathbed final word would be "fish." We went off to different places but have stayed in close touch and visit as often as we can. He is my kindest and most contemptuous friend. I've gotten lots of great postcards from him.

"Ernst Tautenhayn"

My career didn't take off until I met Ernst Tautenhayn. It was Ernst who first taught me how to make shadow puppets other than bunnies and elephants, and how vastly to improve the bunnies and elephants I already knew how to make. Ernst's right hand was extraordinary. With it alone, he could snatch and light a cigarette in a single motion, pick the suitcoat pocket of a passerby, undo the buttons of a silk blouse to a samba rhythm. Ernst was never without an audience; people watched him wherever he was, instinctively aware that his was a life brimming with nerve, wit, and pleasure. Once I resolved to go on the stage, there was no question that he would be my mentor, if only he would have me. Have me he did, as servant (I shopped and procured for him), stage assistant (I hung screens, set lamps, and narrated the shadow-puppet farces Ernst performed solo, shrapneled left hand notwithstanding, a war story he kept fiercely to himself), and sex slave (he had me watch him with men and women alike, it jazzed him and was part of my training). By the time I was done with Ernst, he was done with me. By magic we agreed on that moment. It was after a show for an elderhostel in which, as a warm-up to his act, I shadowed Dürer's *Dance of Death* in scabrous detail without fretting the crowd in the slightest. It was now plain to us both that I could handle any situation that did not require betraying myself.

Ernst Tautenhayn

"Oxford, High Street"

I t was my impression, as the time for my matriculation to college approached, that the world of books and ideas was as limited yet perfect as a sequence of vaulted Gothic ceilings. Does one ever feel confined by vaulted ceilings? Do they not, rather, suggest an amenable upward flow from the limited known to the empyrean ceaseless source of all? I recall a fantasy of strolling down High Street, Oxford, with a tin of especially pungent latakia procured at my favorite tobacconist's. On a whim, I paused to pop the tin with a sixpence and stuff a thumb's worth of the sticky strands into my pipe. The spires of Oxford hovered about like so many perches from which I might take wing. It struck me then that Hegel's idea of the Absolute manifesting in History corresponded to Emerson's view of the Transcendent manifesting in Nature, if one regarded History and Nature as masks concealing the Kantian Noumenon of Existence, which in itself was a mere emanation of Deity. Laughing to myself as I struck a Swan Vesta and puffed at my briar, I quickened my pace to return to my rooms and convey the good news to my porters and hallmates. There was no question that college as I fantasized about it was going to be a fun, interesting place where I would find friends who would understand me finally. And I couldn't wait to smell the old books in the library stacks.

Oxford High Street

93. SIDI-OKBA. — Intérieur de la Mosquée

"SIDI-OKBA—Intérieur de la Mosquée"

It was around the time of my seventeenth birthday, October 12, 1968. I had arrived at Antioch College in Yellow Springs, Ohio. It was called an experimental college, with no grades and alternating semesters of study on campus and work in the real world. It rained a lot that fall and the mailroom in the student union was usually muddy when I came to get what I hoped were letters from my friends back home. My mother sent lots of sweet cards with twenty-dollar bills inside and handwritten notes telling me to have fun and enjoy life. On campus, there was a stray, brown-spotted dog named Muttley whose white fur had turned blue. No one knew how, but the rumor was that Muttley had been dosed with bad acid. The black students on campus decided to live in their own dorm building, no whites allowed, to which the administration agreed. The rumor was that they had guns. My roommate was from a private school out East and had been living away from home for years, so he was ahead of me that way. The local bakery opened specially at midnight on Saturdays with a hot new batch of glazed whole-wheat doughnuts. My roommate and the other guys in my hall made a doughnut run one Saturday but I stayed behind, listening to *Surrealistic Pillow,* smoking hash, and obsessing on Grace Slick singing how I needed somebody to love. I woke up at nearly noon Sunday with a white wax bag of greasy doughnut on my chest, which I took as a gesture of kindness and as a handy breakfast. In dorms and even the gym, guys took showers with their girlfriends. If they were there when you wanted to shower you stayed cool, took it in even, just no staring, not even if you were a virgin. My favorite professors were the old male hold-overs from the days when books were taken seriously. The young psych professor I had for my course on "Perception" assigned optional class reports (coercion would only lead to lying to please the teacher, he told us) on how we perceived the world. Students with long hair and expensive cameras took slides of shadowy flittery nature in nearby Glen Ellen; of foreplay with their lovers; of psychedelic posters in black light; of candles and incense glowing in India brass bowls before Krishna. I chose not to give a report. I tried writing one and it was lies, just like he said, but lies to please my fellow students, not him. I burned the pages in the metal waste-basket in our room and black ash bits got all over my roommate's bed, which he forgave the way you would a puppy piddling. One evening I walked out past the athletic field where all events were coed, un-coached, and intramural and found a set of seldom-used bleachers facing west. I held the book I was reading, D.T. Suzuki's *Essays on Zen Buddhism (First Series),* just high enough to block the setting sun. I don't know what passage it was, but I set down the book, impressed somehow, and the sun, as it happened, wasn't to be feared at all. Its rays were gentle, the fields about me green and tended. Pale Venus appeared in the empty blue hand of the sky like a coin trick. For the first and only time in my life I forgot I was there.

"Almost from Head to Toes"

In Jerusalem, during my junior year abroad, the woman I thought I would love forever and I became lovers. She had come separately to the Holy City after her graduation, at which point she had broken off with the young man with whom she had been in love for most of her college years. In the autumn, by accident, we met in the library of Hebrew University, where I was a student. Obtaining her address and phone number, I persisted gently but obsessively with my attentions. It was fitting for my fantasy of her as a dusky angel nurtured and protected by the gods that she had found lodgings in a single-room garden house in the backyard of an old Jewish residential district. I could walk to it from my dormitory, by way of a semiarid valley. One night, after many shy visits there, we began to kiss and went on kissing for hours, yes, hours. Her black hair fell over my face, a robe of initiation. I was a virgin. My first orgasms with her were in my own jeans as we lay together writhing on her bed. At last, in the hoarfrost winter, we became lovers. Paul McCartney's first solo album was playing in the German Quarter apartment of a friend of hers who was away. We were both fumbly. At dawn beside her I heard the muezzin's call. She was asleep with her rich hair now falling over her black brows and ripening plum skin. It crossed my mind then that if I married her, as I intended, I would never have any other women.

"The Sphynx and Pyramid"

For all the nastiness about the Sphinx in the Oedipus tale—to be discounted as mere Grecian jealousy toward Egypt and its elder wisdom—I found her to be somewhat affected yet sincere, a cross between (putting aside the fright of her lion's body, serpent's tail, and eagle's pinions) a tenacious litigator and a pompous but learned Jungian analyst who insists to her clients that to grow means to pay. Contrary to the Oedipal version, the Sphinx I met was no riddle-poser. Rather, she insisted I speak first and ask the question that had brought me to such desert wastes. The truth was I hadn't planned to meet the Sphinx, I was merely en route to Heliopolis (there to comb the bazaars for old post-cards—that I kept to myself), and had lost my way. But the Sphinx disbelieved in accidents, which she viewed as a categorical falsehood stemming from the fixed-forward gaze of the human cranium. So I asked (with the Oedipal riddle of Man in the back of my mind): "Why do we grow older rather than younger?" She replied that it was a weaning from the physical, to prepare us for the next step, in which a youth of a different kind would be restored to us. Same old same old. I then asked: "Why do we have to suffer to wean?" Through her time-broken lips came this fortune-cookie nightmare: "Because suffering is what you are able to believe."

The Sphynx and Pyramid

"The Kvutzah Watchman"

A piece of advice I would offer to anyone would be not to read your lover's diary in secret. The sense of being entitled to know who your lover is can be dangerous. When I looked into the diary of the woman I thought I would love forever, I found that before we had met in Jerusalem, a young dark Israeli soldier on leave had taken the seat next to her on a bus and seduced her with sizzling ease. The brief affair ended when sex as all there was between them got to her. I became jealous and it lasted within me in secret and open ways throughout our first three years together. Jealousy is a fantasy you conceive because it arouses you. Part of the arousal is believing the fantasy was real for someone else. A man I never met or saw spoke with practiced idleness to her as his breath brushed her ear. The bus was crowded and they were pushed close. She felt herself wet and squeezed her legs together. He got off at her stop and walked her to her door. As she fumbled for keys they set a time and place to meet again some other day but when she opened the door he came in too, wordlessly, shirt open, muscled, smiling.

She started to make tea. He laced his arm around her and they kissed. At first he began unbuttoning her blouse, but she finished that task for him as he was so sweetly and achingly doing everything else. Long after the woman I thought I would love forever was gone from my life, I realized it was me he was seducing in my fantasy. I had become her to feel the pleasure she'd had from a man I should have been.

"Man on Moon"

By the time I graduated from college I was I think what you'd call a fellow who knew what's what. I understood that there were many young men with uncertain prospects like me. I understood that I could read books but couldn't match them up with what was happening about me, an inutility that made them all the more precious. I knew that my girlfriend was as good a person as I could hope to find and that I would have to leave her because I'd been with her too long. I even had an inkling that I would make her leave me so I'd regret it less. I knew I was scared of many things and that over time I'd likely get duller not braver. I decided to be brave while I could by taking chances but not too many—chances in the way of travel, friends, drugs, attitudes that twisted harder than drugs. I saw there was nothing I especially believed and that the meaning in my life would come from keeping busy. If I had a point of pride, it was that I could see that lots of other people were stupider. A searing weakness was that my looks seemed accidental—I never knew if women would like me or not on that score. There were intricate signals to which I was blank; twice I asked out lesbians who were irritated at having to explain. I kept to a long view of things. I would wear people down by avoiding the mistake of cultivating surface charm. At some point before they died and I died, they'd see I was good, fermented cider and drink me down.

"Astronomical Clocks Made by Mr. James Scott"

Precision and acceptance are a rare combination in our species. It was this very combination that I found in Scottie the winter we became friends. We'd known each other vaguely in high school, but six years had passed. Then there he was, in the late-autumn dusk, a lank and towering man with golden hair that brushed his shoulders and a golden beard with a tapered point like Robin Hood. He was standing outside the Starr Bookshop in Cambridge, peering through the window at a marbled leather volume of Rossetti's poems that he could not afford. Scottie had been living in Boston for a year, I was in my second year of law school, but neither of us had taken root in the East. He had the good grace to regard my spewing hatred of the law as the sign of some as-yet-unperceived higher potential. He treated my girlfriend with the deference due the heart of a lady and chided me to do the same. He recited poetry in the voice of a favorite tutor to the angels. At bars he enjoyed his stout and rarely ordered a second and never a third. There was a caution in him that knew the worst lurked, and a charm to him that suspected he could lull it. He worked as an orderly in a hospital, now and then found club gigs as a solo singer-songwriter-pianist. When it got noisy he sang more softly, whispered the lyrics, created a hush for himself and his ballads.

Astronomical Clocks made by Mr. James Scott, the Selkirk Mason-Astronomer.
Scottish National Exhibition, Edinburgh, 1908.

"Una India Centenaria Aymara"

After we became friends, Scottie introduced me to a woman he had met while attending an Episcopal ceremony in a Beacon Hill church esteemed for its beauty and its choir. And though Lettie was more than three times his age and married, still Scottie regarded her as a troubadour would his belle dame. He composed songs of praise and wistful love that he sang to Lettie in her cramped living room in a sagging South Side harbor house on Sunday nights when she liked visitors best. Her husband, who worked in the fish market, didn't mind, though he did absent himself, sitting in the kitchen reading the tail ends of the Sunday *Globe* while his wife conducted her salon with Scott and, eventually, me. Lettie had been a teacher before she retired gratefully to her houseful of books shelved everywhere, including stairways, bathrooms, and kitchen cupboards. Now and then a shoe box of old postcards would interrupt the spines. Lettie served us tea in porcelain cups with hand-painted vines and roses and lovers. We brought her lemon cookies from an Italian bakery she liked. What did we see in her? Beauty that had survived age as ivory does. Sad and gay reminiscences of her books as if their titles were names of dear friends and lovers. A gracious appreciation of our adoration and gallantry expressed in a manner women our own age could never have accepted.

Una india centenaria Aymara - La Paz (Bolivia)
100 years old.

SOUVENIR DE PARIS

"Souvenir de Paris"

n the summer of 1973 I made it to Paris. My plan was eventually to meet up with the girlfriend of a young man who despised me. That young man was convinced that the woman I thought I would love forever should leave me. He was short and built like a teddy bear, with a soft pelt of mustache and the dewy eyes of Omar Sharif as Doctor Zhivago looking out over the snowy steppes composing his poems for Lara. But the young man couldn't write. I could, or rather I would, write, and that was why I was in Paris. It was a further victory to be meeting up with his girlfriend in Paris. I wasn't attracted to her, but I would have loved it if she were attracted to me. We knew we were only friends though and that it was just coincidence we had time and money to go to Paris the same summer, and wouldn't it be nice to hook up at some point and take in the Midi together for company's sake? Meanwhile the lovers we left behind in Ann Arbor commenced a flirtation that stopped just short of consummation, but with a kind of tacit agreement that they would fall to fucking as soon as the centrifugal force of our being in Europe set in fully. Of course, I knew nothing of this at the time. It was my destiny to see Paris as a young man pursuant to the template of James Joyce. I had under my belt *Dubliners, A Portrait of the Artist as a Young Man,* the volume of notebooks and critical pieces edited by Ellmann, and a failed first start at *Ulysses.* Also the ecstasy of hearing Joyce's recording of the final Anna Livia Plurabelle yes passage yes, yes of *Finnegans Wake,* to which amateurs added an apostrophe. The setting was the office of my favorite undergrad writing teacher, an elderly man whom I was, given both me and the times, too stupid to know was gay. Not that he was attracted to me, he had a same-age companion none of us were permitted to meet. He smoked Three Nuns pipe tobacco as the voice of Joyce, a blind, glass-bell voice, reached into my ear like Bloom to Dedalus. My professor had not the first but an early printing of *Ulysses* issued by Shakespeare and Company, the Parisian bookstore run by an expatriate American, Sylvia Beach, who took Joyce on when no one else would. Imagine my excitement when he proffered, through clouds of Three Nuns, that Shakespeare and Company had been purchased by an elderly gent after Beach's death and moved to a new location kitty-corner across the Seine from Notre-Dame. Further, this new owner provided upstairs lodging to travelers in exchange for their putting in some hours shelving and selling in the shop below. Which I did for my first three days in Paris before meeting my friend. Four other young men and I shared a room with a single couch that I was given my final night there, a gesture I took as a sign of friendship or maybe it was just my turn. We were all stinking, as there were no shower facilities. Most of the customers were American tourists hung up on Hemingway and the Lost Generation. By contrast I considered myself an insider. To the French customers seeking help finding English-language books I spoke English as rapidly as possible to revenge myself on the way Parisians spoke French to me, if they spoke at all. Nights, I walked around getting lost in streets with everything shuttered. People speak of the lights of Paris but I remember the shadows and the underfoot screech and burnt-copper smell of the Métro. According to my map, I hiked all the arrondissements, crisscrossed four of the ponts of the Seine, and probably passed at least one café in which Scott and Zelda drank to blackout. When I met up with my friend, she was fresh from the ecstasy of the Breton coast. Together we hitchhiked to the Midi, a straight, south highway shot we made easily. We camped on the outskirts of Cannes and stubbed our toes on the rocky beach. Then we resolved that it was back to Paris where we could split the costs of a decent hotel room and maybe take our time through the Louvre before heading back to the States. We hitchhiked again and this time our luck ran out. Two trucks in the same lane of the same highway stopped at the same time. Two drivers with pomme de terre bodies, on which you couldn't tell what was muscle and what fat, convinced us that it would be more comfortable and conversational for each of us to ride with one of them. Given the times and our stupidity, we said yes. My driver went ahead. Hours passed and I had long lost sight of the second truck in the rearview mirror. When I asked about it, he shushed me like, don't be a child. On his broad dashboard along with maps was a thick, dirty comic book with a masked man in a body-suit who looked something like the Phantom but with a big penis he kept whipping out and using on women in distress. He would rescue them from someone who wanted to rape them and then finally give them what they really wanted. I knew enough French to figure that out and more besides. I thought the driver might kill me and wondered if I should jump out of the truck, but what if I was wrong about everything or I wasn't—either way I couldn't abandon my friend. Finally he dropped me off at an inn and said, when I seemed like I might call the flics, that my friend would be along. She was, perhaps an hour later, and her driver kept the engine gunned as she climbed down from the cab and then he roared away. She had been assaulted but not raped. Her driver backed down when she first screamed and then cried. Maybe, in accordance with how the comic book had it, his erection died when she cried. But it would be his word against that of a young American slut if she made trouble, he warned her. We took a room in the inn. She was afraid to use the shower at the end of the hall unless I stood guard at the door, which I did. As I listened to the shower water I started to cry. When did I stop being young? Then.

"TUNIS—La Rue des Andalous"

We have all had our flirtations with infinite recesses. When I first saw this postcard with its arched disappearances into the heart of the city I was at once within it. The boy leaning his kafiyah-clad head into the studded planks of the door, the ominous, onerous pack on his back—I feel it as biting into the shoulder blades—is either humbly awaiting entry or else too weary to take another step, I still cannot say. Beyond the boy a stranger, an out-of-focus blur, an instrusion in just that way all humanity becomes at such moments as when we wait at doors. What if I were placed on such a street, employed as a photographer for the postcard company? I have been hired for my eye, my daring, my prepossessed anonymity in which I carry a camera as lightly as a cigarette or an umbrella so as to shoot without notice. I offer no help to the boy and keep the stranger strange as I press the shutter.

TUNIS. — La Rue des Andalous. — ND Phot

"Gruss auf dem Cirkus"

first noticed Cara in a class and after that I always noticed her. She was dark olive Mediterranean and her legs and fingers curled like vines around her chair and her coffee cup in the cafeteria. The hold Cara had on me made me realize I no longer loved my lover, who now wanted marriage. I phoned Cara. We had never talked before. I told her that I was in her class, described myself and the row in which I usually sat. It had been on my mind to talk to you but I'm too shy in person, could we have dinner sometime? Cara found it all charming. We agreed on an Indian restaurant in Porter Square. She wore a dark blue pea coat, black stockings, and silver earrings. I had thought it was a bad phone connection, but in person I found that she spoke with a slight lisp, which increased my confidence. We had a nice dinner. She was so flattered; I think I was her first infatuated male. The bad news was that she had a boyfriend and they'd been together for over a year. She wondered if he was really serious, which was why she felt entitled to go out with me. I told Cara I was unattached, which was about to be true. She told me she would like to see me again, but first would have to talk to her boyfriend. A few days later, as we had agreed, Cara called me back. The strangest thing had happened. She'd told her boyfriend about me and he responded by proposing and she had decided that she would say yes. Actually she was telling me before she was telling him. So, thank you for asking and I'll see you in class. She did. We waved. I thought, well, almost is better than altogether never. Beyond that, there was the sense that lust was dust, that I needed to shatter, that a wave of agony was just beginning, that it wouldn't be mine to end.

Gruß aus dem Cirkus.

Miß Bianca

"Le Temple de l'Amour"

Do we all worship at this temple or not? No, not all, some people never love, never fall in love, never trick themselves into it. It's people (or animals you turn into new kinds of people) you have to love. There are two outs people reach for if they can't love people. The first is God, but you've heard the old saying: "Think you love God? Try loving God's creations." The second is things you can count or touch, but as Montaigne wrote: "Whoso hath his mind on taking, hath it no more on what he hath taken." Have I worshipped at the Temple of Love? Yes. I have prayed to be wanted by the ones I loved, not to lose love once I was wanted, and now and then, when I'd been out of the game too long, simply to be able to love again. You can forget how. People forget that. You can have loved and lost, as they say, and then simply forget. The ancients who worshipped nymphs and satyrs were not merely driven by lust and the vine. They were people who knew they had to find love in each other, which meant ceaseless bestial rounds of pain and bliss.

39 Parc du PETIT-TRIANON. -- Le Temple de l'Amour.

" 'Kezon' in the House of Rimmon"

You should have seen me at parties in my twenties, when I could stay up late, was hoping to get some, and was still interested in what complete strangers had to say. I was very funny because half of funny is frightened and I was, by nearly everything, in accordance with my made-up religion that was bits and snatches from all the books and symbols I'd misunderstood. The central tenets of my made-up religion were that life made no sense, that it made no sense because I was too thick to get it (thick physically, thick perceptually, thick above all in the masses of flashing emotions that clouded my mind), but that I still might find enlightenment if I was earnest enough to mess up all my earthly hopes and leave myself no path but the spiritual. This was a frightening faith and it made me funny, because I was always slipping on other folks' seemingly surer assumptions and it made them laugh. What I didn't get—part and parcel of not getting things in general and being so funny that way—was that they liked their assumptions slippery. "For God's sake, man," they'd have said if I'd been insistent instead of funny, "the last thing we want to believe is anything sticky. We like what we want and we take what we want and become something different once we've had it and after we've had enough." So I was funny, as I didn't know what I wanted and wasn't getting enough of it either.

"Tower of Silence"

Returning home after dealing with people, I have the sense of silence rushing at me as I unlock the door. There is the same brief echo of turmoil as with water just gone down the drain, and then nothing except for my own noises that I don't hear. There is the hot silence of summer with the windows open and the curtains lifting now and then like idle hands reaching for an apple, a magazine, a smoke. There is the cold silence of winter in which the frost webs the panes and the telephone shivers as it rings unanswered. The deep, daily silence of single life seldom survives the decision to marry. That was the loss for me, not monogamy. A couple reading together in a room is a comfort, not a silence. Being a parent and loving your child means giving up silence when the child needs to break it. You cannot recover your silence through anger, a corrosive. Stepping back into silence is now a fantasy, as in the old tales when one stepped into Faery unawares, nothing changed so much as lit from within. I've often contemplated climbing the steps to the lasting Tower of Silence but then grown afraid. I fear that it would be weakness—evading the world. I fear I would contract what the monks called *acedia,* dryness. I fear I would worship my own hallucinations. I fear that one night I would jump the wall and hire a whore with coins stolen from the alms bowls of my brethren.

Tower of Silence, Bombay.

"Young Man with Rifle, Black Dog and Dead Ducks"

ecause my parents survived the Holocaust as Jewish par- tisans hiding and fighting in the woods, it was important to me to prove myself in the woods as well. Not to them, but to me. I arranged for immersions, spans of ten days or longer in which I was carefully, minimally equipped for wind, sun, rain, the wet of the northern Minnesota Boundary Waters—ceaseless intricate chains of lakes ranging in shape from Australia to fallen leaves. The only problem was that if I'd tried such trips by myself I would have died. I had no idea how to pack, paddle, portage, pitch camp, produce potable lake water, plot an ultimate course. My friend Greg knew all these things and more. He could balance on the gunnels of a fully loaded canoe in the middle of a lake on a windy day and arc a pee away from us. He could scout the depths and shallows of a rocky shoreline to find a safe site to dive into naked over and over, cutting through the throbbing sun of July into water that was ice only two months before. He'd been going to the woods since boyhood and had a feeling for it I stole from. He loved to bathe in the lake with biodegradable Dr. Bronner's eucalyptus soap while the morning sun was still caught in the trees and a tiny cassette player floated out Northumberland pipes or the Grateful Dead. I'd ask what should we do today, he'd say, "Let's get lost."

"Northern Pacific Caboose"

Of all the jobs I've had, I most enjoyed my time as a railroad lineman, especially enjoyed those lazy afternoons in the caboose waiting for the freight cars to be loaded so that we could be off on our way over the Rockies. A caboose—now all but obsolete—was a little boy's clubhouse made adult and placed on wheels. There is every bit as much play in putting the pot on the coal stove as you ascend the Montana timberline as there was in the Cowboys and Indians of my youth. The English historian Walter Bagehot once observed that work was the most enjoyable of human pursuits, though it did not look like it was. Well, the railroad looked like it was and it was. You could wear old clothes. You learned to couple and uncouple cars and it was like playing with a giant's toys, though if you got careless, as some did, you pancaked your hand and retired to a shanty home on a stinking pension. You could roust out the hobos riding the rails or—if you took a liking to 'em somehow—you could invite them back for a square meal in the caboose before escorting them off at the next town. Land was something you rolled over. Time was the steady pull of the locomotive. You hand-rolled your smokes and shared your whiskey in the off-hours. You slept and spat and shat together in the caboose. The men you worked with knew you as a man. Train whistles were prayers.

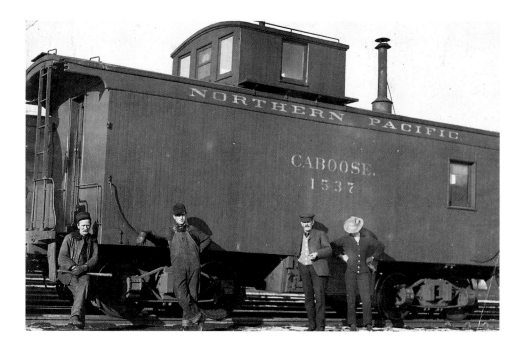

"Standing Young Guy with Bow Tie"

When I first embarked on a career in the rhetoric of commerce, it must be understood, in order to understand me, that I was quite unable to commission a tailor to properly cut the length of my trousers, nor could I long stand upright without groping for a table against which to balance myself. The closer someone came to standing directly before me and speaking, the more surely a vertigo stole upon me, a panic that I could suddenly fail to understand this and every other insistence of this world—could snap out of orbit, a mere asteroid. The greatest isolationists are whole planets unto themselves, with teeming flora and ranging fauna and eclipses timed to the movements of their souls and the gravitation to draw toward them what they lack. That was what I wanted to be, my own planet. How then was I supposed to do business without looking slightly elliptic? I was sneaking about, trying to pass, urgently occupied with matters I thought better left undone. I thought in secret and only in secret. The rest was learned patterns adapted to conclude what was needed. One lunch break by a fountain outside a big bank I read Petrarch's letters. Someone wrote him asking why he'd given up the practice of the law. Petrarch answered that he could not turn his mind into money. My problem was I thought you had to be a genius to justify not making money your mind. That you could die from doing that was something we all had to do.

"The First National—Soo Line Building"

By the time I worked in the Soo Line Building, the First National had given its name to a new and taller building. As for the old building, it no longer seemed, to me, quite so much illuminated as lit up. I could see, but a great deal was hidden from me personally. I worried about getting stuck in the elevator after it happened to three people for two hours one afternoon. It wasn't funny, you could sweat in there. And then you'd have to work late to make up the time, which, to my way of thinking, was all the more irretrievably lost. Some of the men who worked for the Soo Line back then wore toupées the way they wore ties. You want a tight cloth around my neck, here's a tie. You want strands on my head, here's a toupée. They were doing their job and you don't jeer at a man for doing his job because it looks like roadkill on his head. Hell, I had nightly lint goo between my toes from the dark socks I wore with my suits.

The First National—Soo Line Building.
MINNEAPOLIS.

THE TALLEST BUILDING IN MINNESOTA. THE FIRST NATION-
AL HAS GREATER RESOURCES THAN ANY OTHER BANK WEST
OF THE MISSISSIPPI RIVER. ENTIRE BUILDING ILLUMINATED
WITH SUNBEAM MAZDA LAMPS, FURNISHED BY THE WEST-
ERN ELECTRIC COMPANY.

"Chinese Elder in Doorway with Book"

There was an older man who worked downtown while I was a younger man who worked downtown. He was gay and well read and in love with my friend, even though he already had a lifelong live-in companion. My friend was not gay but liked this elder man very much and took to spending evenings at the apartment of this man and his companion, who seemed to have put on the widow's cap as far as sex was concerned and enjoyed serving tea with lemon or sugar or milk. The elder, well-read man was giving my friend what amounted to a series of salon lectures on delicate British mystical byways such as AE's *The Candle of Vision,* David Lindsay's *The Violet Apple,* and the assorted Theosophists. This was partly to my friend's taste but very much more to my own, and after a time my friend suggested that I come, too, and I was welcome because I was happy to listen and upped the odds that my friend would keep coming. It all ended when I invited the elder man to contribute a book review to a pointless journal with which I was involved. He wrote the review; I asked, in what I thought was a nice way, for a rewrite that would state more clearly what he meant. He did not do the rewrite and we never spoke again. My friend stayed out of it but stopped his visits after a while because he found a girlfriend. I would have liked to have kept coming.

"Smartly Dressed Young Man"

Fitzgerald thought the rich different from you and me. Sometimes that is true. Money and careful attention to breeding can produce a person of exceptional clear skin and grace. There are as well other ways. My friend Bob was born into an Irish Catholic family with eight children. His father was a retail-furniture salesman in the days when salesmen knew and believed in their product lines. The three brothers shared a common attic space in which they cudgeled and cajoled each other until they left home. Bob emerged a young man of angular but easy good looks, earnestness, and wit, a taste for faintly wicked pranks and sidesex, an underlying gentlemanly decency and calm. He was among the first males to attend Vassar. In our late twenties, when we became friends, no one who knew us both understood why. We were not opposites so much as skew lines. He owned a little yellow MG convertible I could barely fit in. Yes, we were both writers, but his subject matter was the borderlines of clarity and mine the chasm of chaos. He delighted women and I accustomed them to my routines if they chose to be patient. Drunk, he would recall his Catholic schooldays and his fantasy of pounding down brews with Saint Thomas Aquinas as they got to the bottom of things. Unknown and scarcely published writers, we were to give a local bookshop reading and decided to create a poster for fun: a photograph of the two of us in black tie and dinner jackets, champagne glasses held aloft, him smirking, me sulking, the masks of comedy and tragedy. I eventually slept with a woman I met that night so it was a good reading. It was becoming apparent to me through Bob that the best friends in my life were people who would let me be in their company and somewhat copy them.

APOLLO E DAFNE
Bernini — Mus-V. Borgh.
Roma

"Apollo e Dafne"

There was once a woman I loved who wanted to be my friend instead. We met while we were both working in the kitchen of an alcoholism-treatment facility. We cooked, served, and cleaned on the same shift four days a week. The fifth day I worked with some guy I was glad was nondescript and no competition. The woman's name was Evelyn and she had a supple body like the Queen of the Fairies grown human-sized. I could imagine her with wings. Her eyes were pale blue and her hair was honey blond. We had a lot of time to talk, working in close and isolated quarters but for meal times when the line of alcoholics came past the serving counter where Evelyn and I served cafeteria-style. They could get as much food as they wanted, and it was great food—the freshest fruits and vegetables, bloody little filet mignons and other succulent meat and fish flesh, ketchup and salad dressing without white sugar, whole-wheat breads and cookies. Evelyn was amazed at how sad they looked as we gave them this stuff. She understood that they were sick but she hadn't realized how drained of joy an alcoholic was during the first weeks in treatment. To me it seemed fairly obvious that if you'd just drunkenly fucked up your life and probably lots of others it would take awhile to revive the gourmand within. But Evelyn's dear heart and faerie glamour had me reeling. I could tell that she liked talking to me and that, as time went on, she was telling me everything on her mind. There was no mention of a boyfriend more recent than college three years before. But it bothered me that Evelyn seemed to be concealing nothing and was making no effort to invent herself anew to please me. That's what I was doing when I was talking to her. We finally went out for dinner together one night after work—picking an unhealthy old neighborhood greasy spoon as a kind of joke, as if we were going on vacation from our job—and I told her when we were done eating that I wanted to ask her out for real. Evelyn was embarrassed. She liked me so much but hadn't expected this. She wasn't seeing any men and she wanted to be my friend. Well, if she liked me so much, I asked, what did she like? My mind, she said. The way I thought things through in a way she didn't and probably really couldn't.

It dazzled her that I could do that, really. Thinking things through, as Evelyn called it, seemed to me to be perpetually useless, even assuming I was really doing that, which was her view of things, not mine. I wanted her to love me or want me or whatever you called it. She took my hand and said she was sorry. It wasn't much fun working together after that, and within a month I quit, stealing a box of filet mignons my last night. It hurt in a quiet way for a long time. A year later the phone rings one night and it's Evelyn. She says her name and my heart pounds. She wonders if now we can finally be friends. She has waited a year to let me come around to that. She can't see, I know, that she's insulting my love, so I hang up on her without answer.

"Chimère"

The gargoyles come out thickest in the middle of the night when you're lonely. Everyone knows that. No one denies it. How much of life is devoted to trying to sleep through the night and not be lonely? When there is no longer refuge in solitude or rest, you are enduring the greatest mental pain you can muster all by yourself without resort to violence. It got to the point for me that gargoyles in my dreams woke me up by telling me in a deep dream voice that they'd be there when I woke up, too. They weren't, of course. I wasn't crazy. But as I'd just dreamed about them, they were running around inside me and staring out of my eyes in the middle of the night. That much was pretty difficult to explain away, as there was no one to whom to explain. I had lost the woman I loved just weeks before and was now losing sleep, the will to keep my job, the ability to look into a mirror without panic. Drip drip went the rain down the scaly backs and claws of the gargoyles. I was taking Valium I'd stolen from my father's prescription supply. Valium didn't keep me asleep but it let me wake up without thinking first thing "She's gone!" in a gargoyle hypnopompic voice spoken from inside. I tried reading but my brain set fire to the pages as it did to music in midair. The turning point—it took months—came when I knew I needed sleep more than I wanted her back.

Série II. 5 I-E.B.   PARIS.—Notre-Dame.—Chimère.   ND Phot

"Two Pretty Darn Happy Brothers"

verything I know about the film business I learned from two young brothers who worked down the hall from me in the early 1980s. I was about to quit my office job. Nervous and vulnerable. Susceptible to an offer to return to show business, particularly if the offer was made while I was taking a pee. In our common hall bathroom, the younger brother washing his hands said, "We've been meaning to ask if you'd be in a movie we're making." Naturally I snorted, but within my heart thumped like I was Lana Turner on a drug-store-fountain stool on Hollywood and Vine spotted by the agent who would make her a star. The two brothers were working for their dad's real-estate-appraisal business, and to reward them for their stick-to-itiveness the dad was willing to front a video script they'd written and wanted to shoot. I met with them later that week for a drink after work. It was a spoof on Invasion of Earth–type pics. They called it *Aliens from Elsewhere*. They'd make it on the cheap using actors who would become very limited partners in any profits made from direct distribution to video-rental outlets.

There was warehouse space for interiors. Exteriors would be shot on the streets of a small depressed Wisconsin town that agreed to rent itself out entire to the boys for one July Saturday. My part, they explained, was that of some pompous world leader who's zapped while trying to negotiate with the aliens. I asked to see the script. They said no way—to keep things spontaneous, no one would see their lines until the day scenes were shot. There were no long speeches to memorize. "This is an action flick!" they said laughing at the same time like brothers. I never believed any money would come of it. But it was a way to get back into acting and maybe hit it lucky with some cult-status piece of crap. It would, at the least, give me something to do while I adjusted to having nothing to do. The first week I sweated in a hot warehouse while the brothers learned to operate lights, cameras, sets, and props. My fellow Council of Earth Leaders actors were amateurs, of course, but they let me bum freely from their packs of Camels and Kools. We roundly insulted the brothers for their dreadful script—doled piecemeal to us like so many pages of stale bread—and for their inability to finish a day's shoot before 2 A.M. Our arrival in Wisconsin was ignored by the town's few visible residents. There was a rotting Mobil station with a rusted red Pegasus screwed to its wall still straining to fly away. The "aliens" I was to confront for the first time on these silent tarred streets proved to be Hmongs from Cambodia. That was the joke, the brothers explained—aliens in the legal sense. And their language would sound like outer space gobbledygook. I nodded and waited until they were busy blocking out the scene. I got in my car and floored it, the continuity of the film lassoed and tied to my rear bumper like a black man to a Texas pickup.

"Hermès d'Anticythère"

A message from Hermes is a rare and welcome thing. Welcome, I know now, even if the content is unfortunate, for there is good fortune of a kind in knowing the will of the goddesses and gods. The one time Hermes came to see me he was without his winged sandals or snaky caduceus. His eyes found and held mine until I understood. On a slim pretext I left the party and met him outside in an alley. It was a summer night with a low moaning warm wind. The clouds covered and uncovered the moon like a game of ghost played by delirious nightfree children. "It may be said once and once only," said Hermes. "Listen well." That was what I intended to do. He raised his hand to bestow a blessing but when he spoke further I could no longer hear. I realized now that the moaning wind was the cry of the moon, that the children were running free in the alley, that up in the party I'd been dancing with a woman I hadn't yet intended to meet and hadn't said good-bye to, so the true meeting, when it came, would be ruined now, ruined. The eyes of Hermes were upon me still and his lips moved, but having seen all this before, he knew it was futile. I caught his last three words . . . "ferried before dawn." They were enough to clue me that Hermes had been speaking of his forthcoming guidance of my death. "It is the pride of my species that we don't want to know the day," I explained to the god who forthwith vanished.

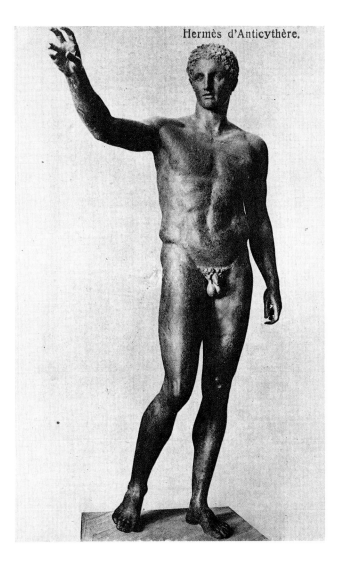

Hermès d'Anticythère.

"Hollywood Midgets"

Oh, I knew it all when I first set out on my own. I'd paid my showbiz dues and learned my tricks and shticks, I thought. It was on a Pullman sleeper between Chi-town and L.A. that I first met the Hollywood Midgets. I couldn't sleep and I kept hearing laughter from two berths away. So finally I pulled up my pants and went to check it out, figuring that as a ruse to butt in I could pretend to be mad at being wakened and then drop that quick if the scene looked fun. It did, and the midgets never once believed I was so much as annoyed. "You drink better than you act," they were telling me an hour later after four guy midgets and I had passed around and emptied two quarts of mescal they'd bought cheap in Mexico with a worm at the bottom of each bottle, which they split and ate like martini olives, and that was where, even smashed, I drew the line. The gals, four of whom were their wives and the fifth (wink wink to me) was lookin', were all asleep. They were all on their way back from a family reunion in Peoria, where they'd walk into restaurants and townsfolk would pretend not to look. A day back in L.A. to rest up and they'd be standing in the Hollywood audition lines again, hoping for parts as bellhops, jockeys, fortune tellers, living dolls, leprechauns, and evil twisted dwarfs gone mad 'cause Hollywood couldn't tell a midget from a dwarf on a bet. There was more call for the guys than their wives, as no one wanted to see a little lady as a victim or a villain. After a while I was drunker than I'd ever been and wasn't shy and asked if they had any tips for me for getting work. "Sure," one of them cackled, "lose three feet." "But I've only got two," I answered, not getting the point as deeply as I have ever not gotten the point. The midgets went hysterical slapping themselves to keep from laughing so hard they'd puke up those worms on their bed. Fine, I finally got it. I told 'em good night and slid out of their berth and nearly fell face-forward on the way back to mine. Once I somehow made it down flat I grabbed the sides of my mattress afraid I'd roll out of bed and out of the train and off the Earth into space. Pulled into L.A. a stinking snoring heap hurried off the train by the conductor. It was going to be a long hard climb to stardom.

E-510

"Signed Lovingly"

I think of her as someone on whose shores I landed unawares, merely lost. I was passionate from the outset but first thought her beautiful in parts, eyes, breasts, mouth, blond as wine, voice the moaning shade of the cigarettes she smoked as though she were having sex. It soon swooned together for me and she was beauty whole, sky, water, trees of a Northern lake a frame for her form as we walked Superior shoreline rocks, me with a backpack with bread, cheese, bottled waters, cigarettes, and books. She was Calypso to me because she conducted herself as a goddess, the ultimate cove for a man weary of the voyage, the thickly flowered perfume she wore daily a garland to her grace and naked softness. She was Circe as well for she enchanted me with the dream that I belonged there with her. She was as fond of putting words down on paper as I was, but hers were laments, prayers, and warnings, mine more tentative, epistemological, lurid. She had a photo of herself as a young bride in her bedroom. She was a dove, a doe, a haunted one who haunted you. How could she bear to look at herself each day in that frame, so unattained and unattainable? I don't keep old photos of myself in sight. She liked my bare arms when my sleeves were rolled up. She liked the way I made tuna sandwiches creamy with mayo, which I don't do anymore. She liked my mind, my humor, my fierce little writer's ways, my dog, my old books. I met her children and they were charming and it mattered not to me that I might care for them someday, why not? With their mother I ranged about in a cultured heat of appreciation for her writings and flesh. Oh, I was a daring critic of her work, no mere mouthpiece. Off on vacation with her children—it was talked about between us that this was too soon but that next year I could come along, too—she sent a letter that somehow disturbed me. I don't remember how. I called her long distance. My voice had an edge I don't remember either. That edge was the start of the end of everything. Anger she could not bear. I had not known, she had not said. If she had, I would have, given my state of mind at the time, chained my tongue to my heart in obeisance at her knees. She and her husband had never quarreled harshly. I didn't believe her, I asked her to repeat it: never.

That's when I knew that the cow had kicked over the pail. She was willing to try a bit. We saw her therapist together a few times in an office in an old desacralized church at the bottom of a steep hill. For me, the therapist had something of the effect of a dehumidifier, leaving things between us less dense but drier. She keened now of past breakups with men: "They all say they love me still. They all want me back." Apparently one of them had thought of ending his stay in this realm. It scared her, like she was Deirdre, men falling and dying for her. It scared me, too, that she was putting me in that list already. I promised her that if we ended I would be all right. She told me she would let me know if she changed her mind. I asked her if she ever had before, she said no. Two months later a mutual acquaintance called to find out if she was right that I was suicidal. I wasn't, but I was sick from it, sleep and appetite screwed up, the will to do anything but watch and soddenly hate TV gone. But getting that call made me furious. I screamed curses, kicked doors open and shut, relished the rage that would have been mine no more were she still watching. Me, the son of survivors who'd gone through Holocaust hells, me, take my life for the sake of her, she at my graveside weeping tears of tragic delectation, never, no. At that time I had put up a wide woven Mexican hammock in my porch. The neighbors could look in through the screens at me. To settle myself, I rocked in it and realized she was right, we were wrong for each other. I would have given head to Satan to be wrong just then.

"Making the Largest Chain in the World"

It isn't the weight of the chain, it's the persistence. Age watches youth try to break off. *I want to make my own mistakes* is the voice of youth with time to tack, to brood, to link in season. The voice of age would just as soon end the chain as listen to disconnected advice. I've made the world's largest chain and you have, too. At the times I was making it, I thought I was falling in love or testing out truth or sighting constellations. I thought I was assenting to be kind, dissenting to be wise, repenting to be saved, laughing at the wrong times so as to be avoided by all with a mind to slipping the chain through the ring in my nose that grew there as I stood in the shadows of the forest a short sprint away. I could easily have escaped. I would have if I thought one person, just one, might have wondered and followed—either a woman I loved who would stay with me through autumn-leaf fall and the cobwebbed cold of winter unto the edge of death, or else a perfect master out to capture and teach me, then cart me back to civilization for display, as highly enlightened and awesomely reluctant as King Kong. I played with the chain in my hands while it was still slack. Then it tightened, tugged me, and I was led away gladly. I was going to be able to write books, raise a family, and keep up with advances in human thought after all.

MAKING THE LARGEST CHAIN IN THE WORLD, 3 3/16 IN, LEBANON CHAIN WORKS, LEBANON, PA.

"Walt Whitman Hotel"

According to the back of this postcard, the Walt Whitman Hotel has 200 rooms, 150 baths, parking facilities, an air-conditioned coffee shop, and a cocktail lounge. All this information makes me wonder what kind of hotel I would be. I'd start with a spacious lobby with vast, thick Persian carpets and wing-backed leather chairs in which you could sit unseen. Accoutrements: brass spittoons; marble ashtrays; a mahogany desk with a fountain pen, monogrammed LS stationery, envelopes, and blotter in place; a newsstand owned by an old blind guy who can tell from the ring of the coins on the counter if you've tried to cheat him; a dark, narrow bar with windows positioned to view the sunset; young buff male bellhops in tight scarlet jackets and slacks with brass buttons, golden epaulets, and pillbox fezzes; a reception desk with a brass service bell from Tibet that silences all talk and movement when it is struck; a woman in a grey woolen cape leaving a handwritten note for me at that desk, which the impeccably suited manager hands to me two hours later when I return from a meeting that has settled my future. I ascend in the Art Deco elevator papered in a lime-and-white pattern of rushes and swans aswim amongst them. The note is from the one I loved before I found my hotel. It's the first time she's written since she broke my heart. I reach my room—Number 18, the number of life—and insert the pronged golden key in the lock that turns like a mind on itself. My room is empty, I sleep naked on a pile of blankets on the floor, the heat turned up high. Every morning, room service brings me clean clothes and picks up the old I've left outside my door. I order food and drinks whenever I want. There's free ice in the machine at the end of the hall. Some nights I sneak down there naked except for my bucket; some nights the guests catch me at it. My hotel, though. I float her note unopened out the window into the night. I try but I can't even hear it hit.

"The Monkey Dancer"

When first I viewed the man with two monkeys in chains on a street in Calcutta, it set in mind issues that have since obsessed me. I wanted to see him make the monkeys dance, to see how he and they did it. I also would have wanted to see where they lived and if the monkeys were freed of their chains at night, for surely they would not run away after so many years and perhaps they even cuddled with the man who loved them as a man loves what keeps him alive. I also wondered if thinking the man cruel for keeping the monkeys in chains and yanking them to dance was itself a cruelty, given all that I could be said to be keeping in chains and I didn't even want to start on that, but apologies to all my pets and girlfriends and to my sorry little soul I let out for walks in the park. And if my life is in part a desire not to wind up on the streets of Calcutta, then how far away do I need to run? By the way, I look like a monkey and have done my time dancing. So I had to toss a coin to the monkey in the white cape who picked it up and gave it to the man who put it under his checked turban, then shook his belled rattle. Say what you want, it had a beat, you could dance to it, and they did. I learned that I could watch almost anything if I thought it would leave a memory I wouldn't understand or tire of.

11. The Monkey Dancer.

"Comedy Troupe"

My late-twenties was the last time in my life that I had sufficient confusion and energy in me to try anything. This particular anything was a radio show on a newly established ten-watt community FM station in southeast Minneapolis. Six of us, four guys, two gals, all hilariously funny, decided we'd put together a radio-comedy group called Headcheese—skits, weirdness, improv, sound effects, Little Feat bumper music, that kind of thing. Buddy could do wacky voices and invent great names that had never existed before like Zic Nadn. Greg was conceptual helium without the high voice but with the floaty feel; he was also our sound/techie dude. Peter, who left us after a short time, had the hoary humor of the troll who lives under the bridge. I wrote a lot of skits, including a takeoff of the Hope-Crosby Road pictures called, "Road to Complete and Certain Doom Starring Bob Doom and Bung Crispy." Rhesa could do sassy black mammies, whiny Jews, *Cosmo* bimbos, and also could carry a tune as far as we needed it to be carried. Nancy, who was married to Buddy, had a voice that could go from a chronic sedated lull to a high, happy-little-girl shriek of surprise in a second. Our debut time slot was 10:30 Sunday nights. The studio was in the wooden steeple of an old church. We would do live shows that we taped off the radio at Greg's place. After the show, we'd all go back there and listen to how we did, usually laugh ourselves sick, then go home and to bed maybe 1:30, wake up 6:30 Monday morning and go to work. The low-paid, young, earnest management of the publicly funded station thought we were smutty and immature but couldn't kick us off the air without a long formal evaluation process no one wanted to mess with, given it was only late-Sunday night going down the tubes. On the air our defiant slogan was, "Community radio as you feared it would be." We did bits like Buddy as El Don Doday saluting the latest best-selling memoir *I Am a Cake* by Zsa Zsa Bolwembe. We sent Rosh Hashanah greetings to Pope John Paul George Ringo. In a tribute to homespun regional radio, I received aural oral sex from a dog we falsely professed to be Garrison Keillor's pet poodle Fluffy. New Year's Eve was a Sunday that year and we got smashed, live, in the studio on Jack Daniel's, falling down giggling, reaching over each other trying to hog the mike. Late in the night we offered to send a buck to anyone who would call in and say they were listening. No takers. Still we knew we were good and figured maybe with the tapes we were putting together we could pitch ourselves for a higher level commercial showbiz gig, get packaged. All of us were dying to give up our day jobs. To polish our craft we devised studio space in Buddy and Nancy's stone storm cellar with old wooden doors that opened from the back of their house like wings. We produced some work that still makes me laugh when I think of it. But then pressures emerged, just as in the early days of the Beatles' breakup. Greg thought he was more committed and doing more work than, say, me. Rhesa's marriage to a doctor named Shuggie gave her roots outside of show business. Buddy and Nancy had a kid. Somehow we lasted eighteen months. Greg has all the tapes archived and, like old vaudevillians who've been through the mill of the bookings and rails and flophouses and wind up in the rest home, we all get along fine and dandy now.

"Two Guys in Hats, a Stogie and a Dog"

I t was 1980. I had a steady job I hated that paid enough to purchase my first home, a 1937 stucco with a converted attic second floor and a back porch in which I hung a woven Mexican hammock. The dog came free, an unwanted pup from an illicit hump between my boss's sheepdog bitch and a roving malamute. I called Henry a "mutasheep" and he piddled all over the lima-bean green carpeting that I eventually pulled up in favor of the hardwood floors underneath. My roommate Greg worked behind the info desk at the newly built Hennepin County Government Center with its open space slit up the middle like a toaster, which made it a favorite jumping place for people wishing to end it all in a fall from the twentieth floor to the lobby reflecting pool. So they put up Plexiglas and netting. First night in the house, a bat flew over my head. I was asleep in the dining room, my bedroom filled with boxes, and when I awoke from the flap of the bat I sat up screaming and knocked the crystals off my chandelier. Next day friends came by and took a picture of us on the front steps. Henry was my baby but he wouldn't hold still. Then someone gave me something to smoke and it was all smiles. No housewarming bundt cakes arrived from the neighbors, who didn't much care for single guys moving in. When we came and went they'd stop their yardwork to count and wonder when, with whom, how long, why.

"B & B Bar"

These are some of the guys I knew way back. On the far left, in the cap, was Leo, who was pretty happy all his life but would never say why. In the white hat was Dickson, who looked as if he wouldn't hurt a fly until one day I saw him kill a fly with that very hat and put it back on his head. Fluttering there in a double image with a caftan is one of the Lamed Vavniks, the hidden 36 righteous ones for whose sake God refrains from abandoning the world. Pete, with the big black mustache, beat the crap out of all but one of us once or twice, the Lamed Vavnik included. None of us bore a grudge because Pete got over it quick, never gloated, and bought us drinks for days afterwards as if to say, "What the hell do I know?" Hughie, in the center with the suspenders, was a boring drunk who could have cared less if we all died. The barkeep was Timothy, who was the same with everyone so long as you paid cash. Joe with the slouch was part Italian, part Indian, part whatever else he felt like being depending on who he was drinking with. It was good policy not to keep track of his heritages for him. Still, Pete beat the crap out of Joe, too. It was Seldon on the end in the long coat whom Pete stayed clear of the way even a wolf shies away from strange noises in the dark. One night we were listening to the Victrola and Seldon says to me, "You get lonely sometimes but then you just stop believing it."

"Slight and Pensive Woman"

When the time came for me to make the most difficult decision of my life, which was to give up my day job and devote myself to show business, the only person who tendered the response I needed was a woman of letters named Mary Logue who said simply, "Good." Mary and I have always had terse conversations, ever since she picked me out as someone she wanted as a friend while we were taking an evening writing class in our mutual midtwenties. Mary has a body as lean and a manner as pointed as a scrimshawed whale tooth. She started talking to me as I left class that night. She talked and walked with me for over a block, which was odd as I had never spoken to her before nor ever expected to. She kept talking to me every time she saw me, always with a low, even, probing voice, so that I was tamed into being her friend. We were soon telling each other nearly everything and using the other to test out the waters of our capsizing lives. This meant she had to listen to me complain a lot that I was no better than a filthy, frightened, no, terrified whore. So after some years when I quit she said, "good," because we were finally done with that.

"When the Gentle Breezes Blow"

I was on the fringes of show business and destined to remain there forever, no hope of a catapulting leap to fame or even of ceasing to hear my parents' voices calling after me as I walked down bare dangling electric-bulb backstage hallways in hopes of a break. I wanted to keep working, that was the mainline hit for me. I'd take crummy gigs to develop my skills and there's nothing wrong with that. I took the word "art" into the back alley, pulled a gun, and told it to drop to its knees. I fired and it bled laurels, oils, oboes, alexandrines. Its bowels spasmed and out came all the avant-gardes. I went back to my dressing room, a converted pantry of an old steak joint now a strip club. I poured whiskey on my hair and lit a match. Then figured, fuck it. I didn't need a disfigurement shtick, I could shpritz pure and true and blew out the match. I went onstage that night for a crowd of twenty guys, mostly hammered, and, for the first time in my life, killed. The timing of my punch lines was so perfect the laughs drowned out the drummer's rim shots. After that, it was easy to get paid to tell jokes, which was all I wanted. Sometimes people ask, how do you keep the act fresh doing it two maybe three times a night, maybe 320 times a year? These people are usually old farts catching my act on a cruise ship in which they're shacked in a sardine-can stateroom with a wife whose tits are falling down to her waist. I could ask them how they keep their act fresh, but instead I say: "The joy of it is finding something new in it every night." Because they're audience to me before they're husbands or men. I also don't let on that fresh is the last thing a comic wants. What audience sees as spontaneous is always a gimmick if you're good. You know who my wife is? The female voice of my wake-up calls on cruise ships. You think you wouldn't like a cruise-ship gig? I say audience is audience is audience, brown or yellow or black or red or white, the same, highbrow, lowbrow, same. Their time and money feed the act they want and I need. Everyone has an act to keep going, so everyone everywhere plays their ace, what they have and you want and they need for reasons like mine that I have the guts to shpritz pure and true.

WHEN THE GENTLE BREEZES
BLOW.

"Motel Canuck"

I was researching a book in Orange, California, and staying in the cheapest motel I could find. I would say it was on a busy street but they all seemed to be the same street in Orange. On one corner was a Roy Rogers fast-food place, on another a combo gas station–quik slurp/shop stop, on another a Dunkin' Donuts, and on the last, my motel. It was managed by one of those young very fat guys who has given up. His jeans would slip down to his scrotum as he stuffed used room towels into the washing machine outside the main office next to the Coke and candy machines to which he had a key and helped himself. My room was painted a sickly sea green and smelled it. I bought my own glass rather than use the one the motel provided. There were centipedes in the shower every morning till I figured out to stop the drain at night. I ate Roy Rogers roast beef sandwiches, I ate doughnuts, I drank coffee and slurp. For two weeks I stayed in that room. At first I drove around only to conduct my interviews. But soon I was out on the freeways every night, checking out L.A. junk shops for old postcards, routinely logging seventy, eighty miles a night, prowling in crazy neighborhoods, finding shops already closed. No matter how late I came back, the fat guy was up and the main office TV was on. I'd go back to my room and watch TV, too.

MOTEL CANUCK, 1334 KITCHENER STREET, NIAGARA FALLS, CANADA. PHONE EL. 8-8221
50 ROOMS   -   50 BATHS & SHOWERS

"Le Conteur d'Histoires"

This is what *TV looked like before we got it—a bunch of* people sitting in a circle watching and listening to the same thing. In those days, old people could be that thing if they could tell stories. Old people are pretty much not allowed on TV unless they are being interviewed about money or dying, the subjects on which they have retained an aura of special expertise. Back then an old fart who remembered what had happened once was interesting because you figured it might happen again. Nowadays, only reruns happen again in genetic engineering and computers and TV. There was a pattern in stories that people believed emerged through remembering. The pattern bloomed in your brain like a bush you'd forgotten was growing and now sprouted roses. On TV there's mostly fantasies, not patterns, and the fantasies have to act fast or we click to a new one. The old storyteller carried a staff and coins were thrown into a calabash there by his bare feet. It was like food being made for you, you didn't just take your story, you paid. TV is all the food you can eat every day for just about free—that's the fantasy you watch with.

"Herning 'Kasper'"

In the middle of life's course, having just started to write and teach while living with a dog in a house I owned, I found out who I was. I was lazy in the morning and intense into the night. Sometimes I could hear music and sometimes it bounced off my ears, an annoyance. I was neat, things had their place, but not clean. Dirty laundry piled up as did old soup bones Henry my half-malamute half-sheepdog liked to chew. In those years together we probably took 4,250 walks. There was a public golf course nearby and I could let him loose to run in the expansive roughs that bordered a small lake with a shoreline path. I projected my mind into Henry's head, becoming his panting dog self and smelling the pine resins, sunfish corpses, and snack chips the golfers ate as they waited at their tees, running up and down a hill five times in the time it took me to climb it once, pissing and crapping at whim, slobbering in the lake water, shaking it off like a crazed rock 'n' roller, getting to go home and get fed and sleep and wake up and do it again. The stick I threw for Henry to fetch was the only stick in the world he wanted. Sometimes he slept in my bed, sometimes he didn't. I liked that he licked the plates clean before I washed them. I was content to let the dog establish the customs of the household, which was useful to know.

Herning   „Kasper"

"Cascata verso Fanes"

I n my thirties, in the *Boundary Waters, I found a mossy* concavity in a rock overlooking a falls. I sat there reading Evans-Wentz's translation from the Tibetan of the *Life of Milarepa,* the ascetic, poetic, illumined one of the Himalayas. I decided to call my moss seat a *vajra* throne, a throne of lightning, penetrating wisdom. I knew it was all a fantasy, but I also knew that it was as close as I would ever get to living alone in nature until I understood what I needed. In a few days, camping nearby and making time each afternoon for this spot, I had gone through the book, including the hundreds of Evans-Wentz footnotes detailing the lore of demons, hungry ghosts, hells and heavens, swans and snakes and dragons, Buddha bodies of appearance, fulfillment, light. Evans-Wentz wrote each note as if he intended to stick it into a bottle he'd cork and throw into the churning ocean of time. As no one could possibly fish them all out, each note would have to contain everything in its way, as did Blake's grain of sand. It made me feel that being even an unenlightened writer had its solace if you saw all books as notes people netted from the ocean now and then in hopes of finding something that triggered more.

(4S.) CASCATA verso FANES

CLOUDS AT DARJEELING.

"Clouds at Darjeeling"

I t was in 1910, during the exile of the Thirteenth Dalai Lama from Tibet, an exile spurred by the violent extremes of the Manchu armies, that I spoke to the man known to his people as the Precious Protector and the Inmost One. The Dalai Lama was in his prior incarnation, as was I in the body and speech and mind of a British diplomat whose formal authority was limited to India, but whose interests included the North where Tibet served as an essential buffer to any threat of Chinese incursions. I had, during the lengthy inspection tours of British outposts that were my lot, taken as a servant a lay Tibetan refugee, a lad of fifteen, and his natural volubility proved an efficacious spur for me to learn his Lhasan dialect, though I never imagined that I would one day play host to the Dalai Lama himself. The unlikely setting for that event was a way-station bungalow in Darjeeling overlooking a tea plantation that supplied His Majesty King Edward's daily breakfast brew. The Dalai Lama had scarcely escaped with his life. In the guise of a herdsman he had crossed the southern Himalayas, and it was in herdsman's garb that he presented himself to me to request my aid in obtaining asylum for himself and his ragged retinue of loyalists. I noted that he possessed the protruding ears and bulbous skull that are, they say, amongst the signs of a *tulku,* an incarnated Buddha. For all that his people regarded him as a godman he was considerably afraid, though not for himself perhaps. He sensed that this was the second of a series of incursions—the first, he told me frankly, being that of our own Colonel Younghusband's troops shelling and occupying Lhasa in 1904—that would at last threaten the fast isolation in which the most efflorescent of Buddhist paths had taken root amongst his people. My intercession with the Lord Viceroy of India led to the granting of asylum, on the grounds that it would put the right face on the British stance toward Tibet as independent from China, with the Dalai Lama as its rightful sovereign. This favorable result fostered a kind of friendship between us, though I would never claim to have become an intimate, if indeed there were any such in the life of the Inmost One. Still, there were those who made their presence felt. One of these was a Baba who paid a visit to the Darjeeling bungalow that had become the residence of His Holiness, for want of any better and due also to the preference of the Dalai Lama and Tibetans generally for the cooler north of India. This Baba claimed ostentatiously to have learned of the Dalai Lama's exile by way of a vision, though news of it had already appeared widely in the Indian press. It happened that the Baba's communication modes were in all ways unique. For he had taken a vow of avoidance of speech that was yet not silence. Rather, the Baba employed a sequence of grunts, squeaks, cries, and gutturals that were interpreted by a most heterodox companion—a young native woman of striking beauty whose name, I recall, was Durga. It was Durga who translated the Baba's expostulations into a Sikkim dialect His Holiness understood but I did not. As I was supererogatory to the talk of these two eminences, I stood after making the Baba's acquaintance and asked leave to depart the Dalai Lama's presence, as Tibetan custom required. The latter requested with a gesture that I stay, though he did not, in so doing, so much as glance in my direction. I interpreted this as a sign of some slight unease and wondered if perhaps the Inmost One feared the Baba as a potential assassin, though both His Holiness's attendants and our own British guard had discreetly but thoroughly searched the Baba and his maid for weapons. Compliantly I sat down again and the dialogue—or trialogue, I should say—continued without my participation or comprehension. I could see, however, that the Baba was mounting in agitation even as Durga and the Inmost One retained their composure. Then the veins on the brow of the Baba grew thick and the sweat flowed down his nose like monsoon rain down a barracks gutter. Still the other two kept their calm. Myself, I should have liked fiercely to strike the Baba down, though I cannot say what made this urge so strong in me just then. Finally the Baba fainted. Durga translated his final thrashings and the Precious Protector, looking down upon the collapsed form, fell to a gentle weeping. Durga and I glanced at each other and decided silently that it was best for us to leave the room. She spoke English—that I knew from our opening introductions. And so I inquired in delicate terms if she was at liberty to disclose any of what had been said. She could, she replied, as the Dalai Lama had specially requested my continued presence. The Baba had argued that long ago the Buddha Sakyamuni had renounced the kingdom of his royal father to discover the Four Noble Truths and the Eightfold Path upon which the Dalai Lama's wisdom yet depended. It was not possible, the Baba insisted, to wield both powers—the temporal power of this world and the vajra power of liberation from all created worlds of sense, thought, and desire. I asked Durga if it was not a sacred compassion on the part of the Precious Protector to lead a people who required a leader. It was just such compassion, Durga replied, that had made the Baba faint and His Holiness cry. To myself I thought it was all merely dispiriting. Indeed, it set me off my tasks and routines for the remainder of the day. But by 1912 Tibetans had rousted the Chinese from their land, due to the chaos ensuing from the fall of the Manchu Dynasty and the ascendancy of Chiang Kai-shek. The Dalai Lama returned to his haunts in Lhasa, claiming that rites he had conducted in

Darjeeling had hastened the fruition of the evil karma of the invading Chinese, thereby providing the hidden spur for their sudden retreat. I meant to visit the Inmost One in his Holy City but instead I died a few months later. Before incarnating as me now, I spent a short lifespan as a baby bayoneted by a Nazi before its mother's eyes. I cannot see her face anymore, or rather, there are more dead faces than I can ever know. I have not had occasion to meet with the present Fourteenth Dalai Lama, who is of course the Thirteenth come to his people again. Our paths have differed. Life is disjunctive if it is anything at all.

"Snake Charmers"

If sex is or can be sacred, then sexual confidence is a blessing bestowed by God or the all-pervading Oneness, as you prefer. The simple knowledge that one is sexual and good at sex is always alluring if it stays simple. Don't we enjoy feeling attracted? Don't we enjoy being attracted back? Watching men good at wanting, meaning those who are steadily wanted back, parallels the lure of the music for the cobra. Men with sexual confidence teach me the sexual boundaries of women in ways I could never track, lacking both the nerve and the opportunities. I learn that what I thought was reserve in a woman was patience instead. I learn that there is an art to the praise of women that includes their bodies as well as their souls. I learn that there is always a time and a place when desire grows sufficient. I learn that innocence lies not in purity but in enjoyment. I learn that after a while we've all swum in the same sexual waters together, that there have been nights of quietly, sadly creeping away from the bed even for men with sexual confidence. I learn that men good at wanting are not necessarily good at anything else, which makes some women feel betrayed. Men don't expect more from a woman good at wanting than simply that. They want more but don't expect it. Women are learning not to expect more either, which will even them up with men.

Snake Charmers

"Thann—Dreaming on the Bridge"

So the dreaming is happening only in English. This is an occult postcard, a cipher to the cognoscenti as to what is truly happening on the Bridge of Life. There is no writing on the back of the card to explain the dream. The young woman is wearing a black-winged bonnet like a butterfly signifying flight of the soul. Her right and left arms are posed in the diagonally flat style of Egyptian tomb painting. The four arches in the bridge frame to her right qabalistically bring to mind Venus, kindness, deep-heart knowledge, love as love on Earth can never be for this young woman waiting lonely on the bridge. But see that her right hand points surreptitiously—even as her eyes scan away—to the third-arch apex or intuitive grasp of the Highest, a sign to earthly passersby, such as those strutting young manly peacocks of the town, that the bridge has been crossed without their aid or recognition. She is on her way to the tower behind her, where, through alchemical sex, she creates a spirit companion worthy of her dreams. The mundane identities of her lovers are irrelevant in essence, but for practical reasons she does prefer the elder married men of Thann. They are disinclined to speak to anyone else of what she asks of them, which is to leave their manhoods behind and to possess her in the name of the God who ravished Mary. They are to hold her gaze as she whispers prayers without waver through her pleasure.

Sur le Pont de Thann.   *ALSACE*   *Thann. — Dreaming on the bridge.*

"Tipos Vascos"

ome people dream of what the world should become. Others are drawn to ponder what it could do without. I am of the latter mind, as is my friend Joey. We've known each other now for forty years and have been fast companions for nearly thirty. We would simplify everything: work less, do without, dream within, desire with care. We talk big but we've taken the bait like everyone else, of course. I've got a family, a house, collections of ashtrays, teapots, and postcards, books enough to topple a team of oxen. Joey's got an apartment with a great sound system and loads of CDs, a taste for Haitian rum and art, for good clothes, for late-night long-distance calls, for Caribbean travels. We act as if we know better though. We're failed mystics maybe. Still, you should see us when we're talking, drinking, riffling concepts back and forth like a four-handed card trick—we can make whole sectors of vagrant reality disappear. And we're two Jews in the way that two Spaniards are two Spaniards are two Spaniards, no matter what else they think. *Lantsmen.* We think we'll still be friends when our teeth are falling out. To write those words is to tempt the fates. Yes, there have been a few bitter times between us, which Joey has been the sooner to forgive. Forgiveness for me is the bow of Odysseus I cannot string (Odysseus, doing so, took his wrath). For Joey, forgiveness is fine wine. Drink or brood. I drink.

"Trapper's Haven"

Winter can kill you. Every animal knows that. People can kill you. Every animal knows that, too. Trappers confront both truths. They say traps are designed to be less cruel these days. I don't want to set them. But I have fantasized about living alone in the woods in a cabin and a world cloaked in snow. I would stock coffee, vodka, bacon, beans, flour, sugar, butter, cocoa, tea, powdered eggs, rice, bone-in hams, peas, tubed condensed milk, latakia tobacco, a lantern-sized jar of chewable vitamin C. At night, rocking by my fire, I'd pour vodka shots into a glass filled with snow. A single shelf of books: Whitman, Blake, Homer, Plato, the Greek Anthology, Algernon Blackwood's "The Wendigo" for when the wind howled, Joyce's *Finnegans Wake* to read aloud when the vodka hit, John Cowper Powys's *A Glastonbury Romance* to worm through all winter, feeding on the savory peat of a dead telesmatic bardic tradition. A radio for music and random human voices. Days, I'd trudge through the snow to my blind fashioned from fallen pine boughs. In my backpack, a thermos of coffee and an old Luftwaffe Leica my father bought off an American soldier after the war. Nearly numb in my parka, I would wait for fur-bearing animals to come. They would sniff out my staying hidden as a sign I meant truce, had evicted the trapper, wanted, clumsy as my gloved hands were, to snap them, catch them that way.

H-15 Trappers Haven in North Idaho

" 'Cyclone'—Gay's Lion Farm"

It is open to all of us to change our names. Why do so few of us do so? Certainly Cyclone the lion must have done so as he grew older, though the marketing people took no notice despite the obvious disappointment of children who came to see what once had been. When Cyclone first noticed that the hot sun drained him, that the kinship of hide and muscle had slackened, that his teeth could no longer tear flesh without pain, that exertion of any kind wearied instead of roused him, that his hearing and sight had faded to the point that photographers had to shout to rouse him, that the leavings of his movements dangled on the old white hairs of his anus, then and there Cyclone betook himself to a shady spot and considered new names. Long did he ponder and many were the monikers rejected with disgust. So Cyclone went into the state we imagine animals can, in which the noose of language is slipped and all is only itself, no thought balloons. The lion that once was Cyclone now is lost to us but for his physical movements, which are few. Feeders bring his meat to his feet. His growl comes from his throat, not from his deep mighty lungs. If at this point he could give himself a name it would be "blood circling slowly in body that lived to feel strength succumb to the comfort of dust."

"Cyclone"

GAY'S LION FARM
EL Monte, Calif.

73

"Dinosaur Exhibit at the Century of Progress Exposition"

There are so many movies in which giant creatures come crashing down city streets, upturning cars, trucks, tanks, crushing the police and the National Guard, bashing buildings just to see the humans fly out the windows like fleas from a scratching dog. I have never been afraid of this happening. My idea of pure, scary evil is a private thing. I don't trust people to want to hear it or to understand. I don't want to hear your idea of pure, scary, private evil either. What could be less pleasant, less forgettable, more of a toxin to continuing trust? But as for understanding, what is there ever to understand about evil? There is nothing more instantly recognizable in the world. People get confused because you can define evil in so many ways. But the truth is that early on in life everyone twitches when they're doing what's wrong by their own lights. You can kill that twitch if you try. But then other things twitch. You can ultimately stop all the twitches if you are the type with things to do that you know you will do no matter what. Those who oppose you are life unentitled to life. You kill and deny the corpses exist, eat from fine china hand-painted with roses of blood. So you see that my pure, private idea of evil has to do with this type and especially how I take meticulous revenge upon them that they comprehend horrifically as it's happening.

SINCLAIR DINOSAUR EXHIBIT AT THE CENTURY OF PROGRESS EXPOSITION

"Il Trono di Venere"

A woman I know once said she hated all ways that men described women's breasts. I have read some fiction written by lesbians and to me it seems they are stuck, too. It is difficult to do justice to what breasts are and do and the impact they have upon people. Look at any magazine stand and count how many covers prominently feature them. These include magazines for women and magazines for men, as both sexes like to look at women's breasts. Many folks whack off to pictures of breasts on the Internet. Astonishing that it has become incidental that they feed babies. As an adult, you can recreate the baby feeling by lightly pressing your face into the cleavage of a consenting female partner. I think the breasts of Venus are so beautiful. They rise gently with her arms as she is robed by her maiden attendants. It seems currently permitted to show breasts but not vaginas. I think breasts are more beautiful, though naturally vaginas are dangerous. But through all the postpathogendoreligioismic wrangling, the breast has stood firm as a sight few could say they wished gone. I think the breasts of Venus have the delicate throb of wings, the fragrance of milk, lemon blossoms, and blood, the softness stone has only when shaped into breasts.

"The One Standing"

I met my wife when she took an adult writing class I taught in the late 1980s. She asked me out the last night of class, which was great. I'd noticed her already: freckled, fresh, relaxed, with golden hair and turtleneck sweaters in which she sometimes hid her face up to her nose as a way of taking waking naps during my talks on the craft of fiction. Later she told me she'd felt safe to ask because I'd worn orange socks—so she knew I couldn't have a girlfriend. All this seems adorable, but in truth we messed up our first three months dating. She was nursing the heart wound of divorce, I was used to women who put mystery and daring into their words. Her writing was simple, she was simple, plus she was attracted but not adoring, and when I said what I thought about things, she sorted my ideas like berries or green beans, some edible, some not, and threw a bunch away. All the same, with her draping fair hair, pale blue eyes and rosy mystic calm after sex, she appeared to me a woman Yeats could have adored. She liked best that I made her laugh but for me that was no great achievement. She had two kids who stared at me thinking this guy might wind up sitting at the dinner table with us, oh my God, and his big slurpy dog, too. So when they all went out of town for a visit home back East, I sent her a postcard timed to arrive before she got back telling her artfully we were through. She returned and phoned me before she had looked through her mail. There was a nothing-matters sweetness in her voice that tripped me up. I told her about the postcard and she thought it was interesting I'd done it that way but did I want to get together anyway? Well, OK. It escalated from that. I saw that she knew where happiness was, in places she was willing to share, and that she was willing to accept love from me in that way. I took pleasure in making up secrets for her I'd never known I had. If I stormed in anger, she promptly closed shop until I rang the bell politely. She was a farm girl, she knew when it was time for old dogs to die, which I didn't. I was allowed to be cumbersome with her children so long as I meant well and kept at it. One night at a school carnival she was a volunteer checking bulky winter coats along with another sweaty mother who said at shift's end: "I get it.

You're the sort of person who can enjoy doing anything." By then I'd understood that, too; what she chose to do she did with the love of rain for earth. By then, I had the sense of having slipped into a garden I'd never seen and yet suddenly belonged in. To this day, I walk in it, amazed that earth gives life to roots that press shoots toward the sky. The secret of my marriage, if it has one, is that I was so benumbed beforehand that everything now—a rainy evening playing Go Fish with the kids, say—elucidates.

"Trio of Travelers in St. Mark's Square, Venice"

When Francis Xavier Nulty was seven years old, a priest in Catholic school told him that if he did not confess with true contrition the host would turn his tongue black. A few days later he tested that out. Upon seeing his pink tongue in the boys' bathroom mirror he cried out, "Hallelujah, I'm free!" Yet he went on to marry a dear, devout Catholic girl, Gertrude, and they had three sons and a daughter, Mab, who blended the freedom and devotion of her parents and understood the truth without a creed. The three of them traveled to Ireland when Mab was in her teens. Before we married, I traveled with Mab to Italy, but as she had told me so much about her parents I often confused the two trips and imagined Frank and Gertrude and a younger Mab wherever we went. At the Piazza San Marco, as pigeons took flight at our approach, I knew that Frank would delight at their cooing unconcern, Gertrude at their nearness to the teachings of the Church, while Mab would spot the mothers and the fathers and the chicks, tallying families out of a mad flock. Gertrude was already dead, but when I met Frank I saw the man I'd imagined at San Marco. His open-armed embrace of my love for his daughter was a sign of blessing to take his place there beside her. There is a joy to unforbidden love, like being tucked into life.

"Father Holding Baby"

I say to you that I have been a good father. The one and only time I slipped hard came when Sarah was just a few months old. My wife Mab had gone off one evening to a meeting. Did the young suckling baby miss her mama? Yes, she did. Was Daddy confident with baby alone with him in the house? No. Shortly after Mama left, baby cried and Daddy fed her a bottle and some soft, blended apricots from a glass jar. It was quiet for a while and baby played with colored rings on a blanket spread on the living-room carpet. Then baby started to cry again and Daddy picked her up and held her and walked with her and cooed to her and kissed her lightly on the top of her head and sang to her in the fleeciest voice he could some Grateful Dead ballads that had always sounded to him like lullabies. He had wanted to be a father someday and had thought he would be a good one because he wanted to be. Baby kept crying. Daddy kept walking and rocking baby in his arms and cooing and singing and trying to keep a smile on his face when it came close to hers. Baby kept crying. Baby kept crying. It was nearly an hour and the crying only stopped when baby sobbed, running out of breath. Sleep, baby. No. Baby kept crying. Crying. The sound of a cry is designed by nature to make you unable to stand it and determined to get it to stop. I couldn't. That's why I screamed at her to stop. Thank God at least I did not shake her. Then, shaking all over myself, I laid her on the sofa and sat across the room watching, but saying and doing no more as baby cried and gasped and caught her breath and cried until Mama finally came home. I was yellow and the baby was yellow and we glowed in the dimness of the house from our strain. I have failed to do a good many things in my life. All of those things bother me still, but none so much as that evening alone with a baby for whom a father did and was nothing.

"North Head Lighthouse, Cape Disappointment"

A disappointment is regret without redemption. Often we deceive ourselves that we are better off, things being what they are, than what they could have been. Or we decide that we have gained compensatorily in wisdom, as with Nietzsche's famous dictum: "What does not kill me makes me stronger." Disappointments linger, making us neither stronger nor better by our own sense of things. Desire is the key to disappointment. If we desired something badly enough it doesn't matter that it was never meant to be. My disappointments in life are that I never played major-league baseball; that I was not a breathtaking seducer of women; that I bridle reflexively at ritual; that my soul is a greenhouse for anger; that I cannot imagine the gods taking an interest in us, not that I deny it may be so. Since reading *The Tibetan Book of the Dead* in the Boundary Waters, I've suspected that the manner and state of mind of my death may, as well, disappoint me in the hereafter.

North Head Lighthouse, Cape Disappointment.

"Tangiers   Moorish Prison"

I have often wondered how I would hold up locked in an isolated cell for life. The design of the prison precludes escape and means for suicide are denied me. No visitors, no letters, no books, no speakers or screens. A high, barred window through which the rain drips and the stars taunt. A verminous cot with the residues of prisoners past. Daily bowls of swill, skin, and bones with a bread crust to dip; bowls slid under the cell door, slid out within a half-hour or taken away. Lips and fingers alone for eating. Wipe yourself on your blanket or your shirt. Once a week, an icy wash in a cistern in the prison courtyard. In that same courtyard the twice-weekly exercise sessions, the only time you see your fellow prisoners. Enclosed in stone walls for years you all look alike. Eyes don't focus, bodies move in marionette jerks, no talk as there's nothing to tell, your memories are like dying flies. What could I remember that would make me happy even if I could never see it again? The face of my daughter. But then I would worry that she needed my help and that she would never receive it. That would be the hell of it. But then, one day, a voice from the street—my daughter singing to my window, to me. My wife has brought her there. They are posing as beggars singing for coins but really they are singing for me. I throw a bone out the window to let them know I can hear. In my cell, alone, my dream.

"Les Belles Plumes Font les Beaux Oiseaux"

To say I have a doppelgänger would be overly dramatic. There is a person, or more than one perhaps, who looks sufficiently like me that people say hello to him expecting me to answer. I've heard about him, or them, from friends who run into, let's say him, at blues bars, or airports, or while he's looking for his flavor of ice cream in the frozen section of the supermarket. These sightings, friends tell me, happen maybe six times a decade but steadily so through all the decades of my life since my teens. That means that my doppelgänger, whom I now dramatize, has changed and aged along with me. Surely he dresses better, but perhaps he has been denied a life as rich in sensibility and incident as my own. I realize by now that I will never be permitted to see him, since if we walked toward and then through each other the polarities of the universe would implode and humankind be rendered into fine ash. But I remain acutely aware that this doppelgänger has the awesome power to emulate my being. If only, as a form of truce or kinship, we could do things in each other's name and stead, he to attend all formal occasions and personal partings for me, I to launder garments and eulogize the wanderings of soul for him.

"Tomb of Rachel"

Rachel said, "Give me children, or else I am dead." God gave her children and Rachel never died. We know this because the Tomb of Rachel lies along the path the Jewish people trod to Babylon and exile. Jeremiah heard her there, heard "lamentation, and bitter weeping, Rachel weeping for her children." If my family has an actual faith, it is the worship of our mothers. My father prays to his murdered mother Sarah, after whom I named my daughter. My mother prays to her murdered mother Cila, after whom my sister Cecilia is named. My mother Rachel became Rochelle on coming to America; it was written down that way by the immigration officer. My mother will weep for us when the times for weeping come, even after she is gone. I will hear her as plainly as did Jeremiah. It is no small thing. It affects how you live, how you hope your daughter lives. If the worst happens, I will hear her crying before my own. It has always been that way—the worst of it her cry.

Tomb of Rachel. Bethlehem. Tombeau de Rachel.

"London. British Museum."

In London to research a biography, I found lodgings in a top-floor apartment to a private residence owned by an Indian family man, who had attended Cambridge and become a successful barrister. There were few personal dealings between us. I was gone nearly the whole of every day, and when I came back late in the evening, I crept up the stairs to which all inner doors of the house were kept closed. For one week of the family's ten-week stay, they went on vacation and I took the opportunity to watch their TV, sit in their garden, and look into their bedrooms and closets and drawers. There was a tidy care and calm to it all. Of religious belief of any sort there was no evidence. In my own top-floor room with adjacent bathroom and shower, there were books and documents galore about the religion of a man whose name still had the power to shock in London. I kept that name to myself except when working in the libraries of the Warburg Institute and the British Museum. The former was open only till six, and so I devoted my evenings to copying by hand from certain rare and restricted texts in the latter. The British Museum reading-room ceiling is an immaculate, sky blue concavity. Its immense leather catalogues have the look of the ledgers of Bartleby the Scrivener. The walk from the Warburg to the British Museum was a short one across Russell Square. I found a small grocery on Museum Street at which I would regularly buy for my supper a yogurt, a Scotch Egg, a fruit juice, and a Cadbury chocolate bar. On a bench in the British Museum courtyard I would eat amongst shameless pigeons. I remained alone too long in a city I came to know only on the Sundays when there was no library open. London grey and low, pubs with old, stained wooden walls and ashtrays jammed with butts, parks with nannies and perambulating babies and elderly gents who spoke gruffly to their newspapers when the stories displeased them. I stared at people who didn't like it. A drunk on the tube mistook me for an Irishman. The only thing that still interested me about the man whose life I was to write was the certainty he felt in what he knew, a certainty that slipped through the sieve of the facts I was finding one by one.

London. British Museum. 56.

"Loader at Dehydrating Plant"

People believe in staying active, keeping busy. There was an old guy I met who went to Veterans of Foreign Wars Bingo every week. "I don't like to play, but they let me do the number calling—that I enjoy." A man my age, a moneyed success in business, told me that after he retired he thought he might take a job as a supermarket bagger so he could talk to new people. I met a couple who spend their weekends together scanning public park grounds with metal detectors equipped with earphones. The most common lost valuables, they told me, are wedding rings. There was a woman who, on Friday nights, would walk over two miles to a coffee house that sold cookies she liked. She didn't sit down with the cookie she bought and check out the coffee-house people. It wasn't people she wanted, it was the long walk there and the long walk back eating the cookie, the calories of which were canceled out by the walking. Someone else goes looking for old postcards at estate sales where the possessions of the dead are priced and spread out for display in their own late homes and everything you pick you wonder, will it cost more by the time you're dead and there's a new sale? Cycles of possession and release are ways not to fall hands-first idly into devilish mischief.

LOADER AT DEHYDRATING PLANT
LAMAR, COLO.

"Disdain"

My love for my daughter Sarah is helpless. She is six about to turn seven. From the time she could crawl and babble she has declared her place in the world as measured against me. It was her instinct to do so, or perhaps was due to a past life and a hard lesson learned there, my wife suggests. On the bright side, my wife adds, I may be fated to heal Sarah through patient submission to her ways and needs. That is a life purpose I can accept. My daughter's first memory is of emerging from the womb and feeling vagina hair tickle her face. A week later, walking with her in my arms in a circle route round the first floor of our house on a Sunday night, I stopped by a window. My baby stared up at me, a soul with eyes in a new place but with an old resolve. At age three, while in the car with the Twins game on the radio, I mention her birthday coming up and would she like to do this or that for her party. Sarah says to me: "You worry about Father's Day, I'll take care of my birthday." Of course, she thinks I'm swell in a flawed way and now and then she adores me. We used to go to the zoo a lot together before she got sick of it. I take her to Native American shops to look at beads in the shapes of rabbits and turtles. I'm always hunting for books I hope she'll like and I've had famous writers I've met like Grace Paley inscribe books to Sarah's future self. Sarah said once that Mom loves her like a parent and I love her like a slave. That doesn't mean I say yes to everything, not close, but I know what she's getting at. Once, as we were walking in the woods, I told her what I thought was a funny story and she said: "Dad, if your whole point is that there is no point, that isn't much of a point." Mom and I alternate reading and cuddling with her at bedtime. At first I used to hope she would fall asleep quickly. Now I'm happy to lie beside her as she asks for stories about my childhood-dog Peaches or how I handled school and parents and other kids when I was her age. She knows it's her life not mine she's leading; she reminds me of that often. But she does want source material of mine to synthesize. When she is unafraid of something I was afraid of, it makes us both very happy.

Han't she sweet

2131 DISDAIN

and your postal and letter

"Mosè"

he horns on the head of Michelangelo's Moses arose due to a mistranslation from the Hebrew of the Torah to the Latin of the Vulgate. Exodus states that "his face sent forth beams." The Vulgate has it that "his face had horns." Horns were also a sign of the Devil, and Christians concluded early on that Jews were the agents of Satan. It went beyond horns that you couldn't see. There were also tails that Jews kept craftily hidden, a he-goat Jewish stench that only baptismal waters could wash away, and enfeebling ailments (Jewish men and women alike were believed to menstruate) that could be staunched only by resort to the murder of Christians (especially infants) and the transfusion of their superior blessed blood. The Moses of Michelangelo is the centerpiece of the tomb of Pope Julius II. This Moses is no longer Satanic, but rather a symbol of the Pope's humility—here lies a lesser prophet than Jesus; one who, like a mere Moses, was denied entry into the Promised Land (of a united Italy, for which Julius II had waged war). There's progress for you. These days there are uneasy jokes in which Moses and Jesus play golf together and Moses has to part the water hazard with his driver while Jesus simply walks over it. At a 1995 book signing, John Dominic Crossan, the Catholic scholar and author, autographed my copy of *Who Killed Jesus?* Crossan concludes that the Roman government did the deed, and that Christ-Killer accusations against Jews were slanders by the early Christians against a rival religion. Great news. Crossan signed the book, "To Larry, with best wishes . . ." I wanted to ask him to sign it, "To Larry, who didn't kill Jesus," to have on hand just in case, but I didn't dare push my luck.

634a: Roma - Mosè di Michelangelo

"This is one of the new pictures. How are you all and have you started to clean house yet?"

I'm their stepdad and they're my stepkids. We tried out different names for those relations early on, but none were any less stiff, "dad" and "son" and "daughter" least of all. Their real dad lives fourteen blocks away and they spend every other day there. You'd think it would make them dizzy, but they started young and the young can ultimately understand anything. Nine-year-old Ceallaigh helpfully cued me, when I couldn't think of an answer to her question, if my own best birthday present ever was maybe a book. Four-year-old Brennan cried a lot when we went places together and I was in the front seat next to Mom. We've all lived together ten years since then. I find myself loving them sometimes like they were my real kids. More often I love them as you might people who hung onto the same raft as you in a storm. In matters of parenting, I try to imitate their mother. They've come to listen to me a little. I fart a lot and they think that's funny. We've traveled together; that's been good and bad both. They've grafted with my Sarah as sister and brother. Ceallaigh's careful grace and unsentimental goodness, Brennan's easy allowance for heart as the essence of things, Sarah has fed on these. I do for them what needs to be done and have been there as secondary balm in most of the worst times of their lives. I think they love me for that.

"Patient Arriving"

When the time comes, I hope I'll be carrying as little mental luggage as possible. Wise to remember we know nothing of what happens, however vividly we've fantasized about it. Whether through Hell or Karma, we associate death with dread justice that cannot be evaded. I think that means death resembles who you are, takes on your own stink and light, is experienced by and is waiting only for you. Before he died William Burroughs used to ask how we all thought we knew we weren't dead already. Back in the 1970s I saw Alan Watts explaining on Public TV that from a Zen perspective he didn't really exist. He'd already died before they aired the show, so it was funny. It's possible we switch between Life (here) and Death (elsewhere) on a daily basis and attribute the choppiness of existence to our moods or dreams. Is the most frightening fantasy of death having no one there to talk to and be with, or thinking that thinking stops? Would I rather die in bed surrounded by my family, or simply in my sleep? Probably in my sleep. I'm still a baby, I don't know if I can die well. What if I screamed to my wife to make it stop just as it was happening and while the kids watched?

Patient Arriving—M. W. of A. Tuberculosis Sanatorium, Woodmen, Colo.

"Peasant Woman from Muntenia"

You. Postcard scribbler. I see you as you see me, as a telling photograph fallen into my hands. Your face and bearing as you have tugged them through life so weary a donkey you hate not only what impedes you now but what you have already borne. You lie and balk at lies and stumble forward to the carrot of lies, silly donkey. You scarcely believe what you can remember and the rest inside you is animal, tamed by fear from youth and by fear again from impending death. Your dreams elude you as a cat eludes the footsteps of a drunkard. Grateful you are to those who have loved you but not so grateful as to forbear cursing them for the pain they have left. You eat too fast, you narcotize yourself with words, pills, smoke, drink, songs, orgasms, fate. Mercy is what you afford to sweeten your sleep. You are the vessel that holds what fills it but cannot pour. Your family believes you now comforted at last. Be comforted, then. And like the Ass of Balaam you may someday be granted understanding and so be enabled to speak to your daughter of the ways of truth as a father should.

"On the Half-Cut Stump of a California Redwood Tree"

My wife and I hope to live in the country someday, after the kids are out of the house and the work slows down. Will we make it? To do so, we shall have to satisfy certain fantasies. My wife wishes to live within sight of a lake or pond or broad stream or creek that plashes as it flows. I would like to live far enough from any neighbors to pee off the porch standing naked on a summer morning. My wife is asking far more than me, as riparian land is expensive. But then I surpass her with my desire that, wherever we are in the country, she must live longer than I do.

541   On the half-cut stump of a California redwood tree.

"Under the Furnace of Heaven"

When I was a little boy—*who knows how little?*—I was conscious that grown men had once been like me. But they transformed into fathers of families they took to parks and sights and fed hot dogs and ice cream. My own father did those things, but mainly he worked long hours at his business and we lacked the gift of playing together. At a Cub Scout winter retreat when I was nine, he hurt his back trying to toboggan with me down an icy hill. All the other fathers could do it, it seemed to me then. Now, as we approach death not so very many years apart in the longer view of things, I see a man who was a hero of the Jewish resistance in Poland before I was born, and whom I only met when he was carrying his immigrant family on his back and showed it. My grandfather Julius lived his last years as a child protected by my father, who prayed then and still does to his dead mother whom he could not save from the Nazis. It was her afterlife voice, in a dream, that led my father's soul to my own mother. My wife looks at my dad, says, see how he clings to your mother, won't go anywhere without her, don't you get like that when you get old. Father, your young desire to write incarnated in me. I write for you a prayer that Sarah your mother beloved of God will hear: When the time comes, bring your son home to you. I pray as well to my own mother Rochelle to remember, again when the time comes, to keep a place beside her in Heaven for my daughter Sarah. There, that's all taken care of. I can go now.

Desert. Under the Furnace of Heaven. Rest in the Desert. 447

AUTHOR'S NOTE

I am grateful to my postcard collaborators of the public domain. I have always wanted to illustrate a book but I can only draw sidelong views of dogs. Postcards have allowed me a means at last. Peace betake all who had a hand in their creation. None of the persons pictured in them are persons I have ever met; even if—in two cases—their postcard names are borrowed, they are not the persons written of in this memoir. Throughout, names and potentially identifying details are faked but for those of lifelong friends and immediate family and major-league baseball players. Only a few of the places depicted in the postcards are the actual places of memory. All the desires and the parts where I get disoriented are real.

This book was designed by Jeanne Lee. It is set in Bembo type by Stanton Publication Services, Inc., and manufactured by Friesens on acid-free paper.

Lawrence Sutin is the editor/author of the memoir *Jack and Rochelle: A Holocaust Story of Love and Resistance* (Graywolf Press, 1995), for which he won a Society of Midland Author Award, a Minnesota Book Award, and a Loft-McKnight Artist Grant. His prior work *Divine Invasions: A Life of Philip K. Dick* (Harmony Books, 1989) was awarded (in French translation) the Grand Prix de l'Imaginaire. His most recent biography, *Do What Thou Wilt: A Life of Aleister Crowley*, is forthcoming from St. Martin's Press. Sutin is an associate professor in the M.F.A. program at Hamline University.

Graywolf Press is a not-for-profit, independent press. The books we publish include poetry, literary fiction, and cultural criticism. We are less interested in best-sellers than in talented writers who display a freshness of voice coupled with a distinct vision. We believe these are the very qualities essential to shape a vital and diverse culture.

Thankfully, many of our readers feel the same way. They have shown this through their desire to buy books by Graywolf writers; they have told us this themselves through their e-mail notes and at author events; and they have reinforced their commitment by contributing financial support, in small amounts and in large amounts, and joining the "Friends of Graywolf."

If you enjoyed this book and wish to learn more about Graywolf Press, we invite you to ask your bookseller or librarian about further Graywolf titles; or to contact us for a free catalog; or to visit our award-winning web site that features information about our forthcoming books.

We would also like to invite you to consider joining the hundreds of individuals who are already "Friends of Graywolf" by contributing to our membership program. Individual donations of any size are significant to us: they tell us that you believe that the kind of publishing we do *matters*. Our web site gives you many more details about the benefits you will enjoy as a "Friend of Graywolf"; but if you do not have online access, we urge you to contact us for a copy of our membership brochure.

www.graywolfpress.org

Graywolf Press
2402 University Avenue, Suite 203
Saint Paul, MN 55114
Phone: (651) 641-0077
Fax: (651) 641-0036
E-mail: wolves@graywolfpress.org

Other Graywolf titles you might enjoy are:

Nola: A Memoir of Faith, Art, and Madness by Robin Hemley

Dead Languages by David Shields

Diary of a Left-Handed Birdwatcher by Leonard Nathan

South Wind Changing by Jade Ngọc Quang Huỳnh

The Stars, the Snow, the Fire by John Haines